QUIT WHINING AND START SELLING!

"*Quit Whining and Start SELLING!* is a significant contribution to the art and science of professional consultative selling. I've written many books and college text books on selling, and unlike most of the books in this space that merely create noise, Kelly gets it. He has lived it and has powerful models that can accelerate your performance immediately. Chapters 5 and 6 are must-reads in my opinion; they nail the foundation for why most people I have seen over the past 25 years fail to achieve greatness. Get this book and read it from cover to cover. Make *Quit Whining and Start SELLING!* required reading for every professional salesperson you know!"

— **Dr. Jeffrey Magee**, PDM, CSP, CMC
Author of more than twenty books (including four best sellers),
and publisher of *Professional Performance Magazine*

"Let's be frank, being successful in sales is about mastering the basics and working with discipline. That's what Kelly challenges you to do. He builds you a roadmap and teaches you the skills you need to drive big success. You'll learn new habits and uncover new ideas for being better at what you do. Stop waiting to get lucky—start crushing it."

— **Dan Waldschmidt**
Business strategist, popular speaker, and author of *Edgy Conversations*,
identified by *The Wall Street Journal* as one of the
Top 7 sales blogs on the Internet

"I thoroughly enjoyed *Quit Whining and Start SELLING!* It is a book you can use as your personal sales coach. Sales greatness comes from working harder and working smarter. The first is up to you; *Quit Whining and Start SELLING!* will help with the second. It has the right combination of personal experience, excellent stories, and solid research. I personally learned a lot from this book; trust me, so will you."

— **Jack Malcolm**
President of Falcon Performance Group and author of *Strategic Sales Presentations*
and *Bottom Line Selling: The Sales Professional's Guide to Improving Customer Profits*

"*Quit Whining and Start SELLING!* is a different book on selling. There is no fluff in this book. Readers need to pay attention to the fast pace of the book or they will miss the wisdom on every page. It's a practical textbook that gives salespeople concrete concepts with real world examples that demonstrate how the concepts should work—or what happens when they are not followed. Study it carefully and become the sales professional your customers want to partner with."

— **Jeff Robillard**
Director of U.S. Sales, Acumed

"One of the things I've always enjoyed in my interactions with Kelly—through his speaking, consulting and writing—is his no-nonsense approach to sales and management. There's not a lot of coddling involved; just challenges and common sense. *Quit Whining and Start SELLING!* is a testament to this approach. It contains plenty of high-level discussion on the conceptual aspects of selling, but it also contains ideas that you can implement—TODAY. Real, practical, usable ideas. Kelly tells compelling stories and you'll find yourself identifying with the good and the bad in all of them. This book will make you think, help you learn, and challenge you to grow. I dare you to read it and not come away inspired."

— **Brad Thurman**, PE, FSMPS, CPSM
Principal and Chief Marketing Officer, Wallace Engineering,
and 2013 President of Society for Marketing Professional Services (SMPS)

"I am so excited about this book. Kelly is one of those people who come into your life and you are better as a result. His experience and expertise in sales is so broad it allows him to transform individuals, teams, and companies. *Quit Whining and Start SELLING!* is the blueprint for that transformation. His philosophy that 'Everyone Sells' has changed my perspective on my own business, and, ultimately, altered the course of my company forever. This book will, no doubt, change your career if you are fortunate enough to read it."

— **Teri Aulph**
Author, speaker, and consultant to Fortune 500 companies

1-on-1 Selling™ Journal

..the companion journal/workbook to
"Quit Whining and Start SELLING!"

The *1-on-1 Selling™ Journal* is designed for salespeople and/or sales managers. The journal is divided into 12 sections, one per month, with each section containing a key lesson that emphasizes an important sales idea or concept. Sales managers can use the lesson each month as the foundation for a sales meeting, and utilize the Action Plan to focus efforts on the idea/concept for the month. Salespeople can do the same on their own, or collaborate with other salespeople to create individual accountability.

In addition, each monthly section contains four weekly divisions. Each week a key thought or sales idea is presented to focus on during the week. With plenty of room to record notes, ideas, monthly goals, and other critical information, the *1-on-1 Selling™ Journal* is the perfect companion to *Quit Whining and Start SELLING!*

This valuable workbook can be used:

- to guide monthly or weekly sales meetings;
- to record monthly sales goals and objectives;
- to record notes or ideas from sales meetings or brainstorming sessions;
- to keep track of ideas and resources for your customers;
- as the perfect accessory to *Quit Whining and Start SELLING!*

QUIT WHINING AND START SELLING!

A Step-by-Step Guide to a Hall of Fame Career in Sales

KELLY S. RIGGS

1-on-1 Publishing, Inc.

For information, please contact:
Vmax Performance Group
104 N. 67th Street
Broken Arrow, OK 74014
www.vmaxpg.com

Transforming potential into performance.™

Cover design by Melinda R. Prescott
Cover photo by Don Kreutzweiser
Edited by LeAnn H. Gerst

Printed in the United States of America.
First edition 2013.

ISBN-13: 978-0-9845245-0-1 (print)
ISBN-13: 978-0-9845245-1-8 (e-book)

www.1on1selling.com
kelly@vmaxpg.com

ACKNOWLEDGMENTS

The product you are holding in your hands would have never happened without Robert Terson, a sales champion whose greatest talent is not his ability to close a sale (which is considerable), but his capacity to make a person feel like a million bucks. Thank you, Bob, for your insight, your coaching, and your encouragement. Your prodding and suggestions are what helped me turn this book into something worth reading. I wish you the very best in your "second" career!

Also, my sincere thanks to LeAnn Gerst for her diligence in the editing process, and to Melinda Prescott for her outstanding design work on the cover. You guys make it look so easy!

I am blessed to have three wonderfully talented kids, all of whom directly influenced the writing of this book. I am particularly thankful for my son, Robby, who has become my first choice for testing out new thoughts and ideas. More importantly, as a successful consultant in his own right, he has now become an inspiration for many of those ideas.

Most of all, I offer my love and gratitude to my wife and best friend of 32 years, Rhonda Riggs. Your faith and support has never wavered.

CONTENTS

FOREWORD

"Have you ever noticed that the last people to get fired from a company are the rainmakers?"

My grandfather asked me this question over 30 years ago. He was teaching me the importance of those people who produce revenue for a company. In the years since, I have learned he was absolutely correct. In this era of increased efficiency and "right-sizing," companies (including mine) are constantly trying to do more with less, but the rainmakers—those individuals who recruit and maintain the company's most profitable relationships—are always safe and cared for.

Reaching the top of the sales profession is hard work, but once you become an effective salesperson and achieve rainmaker status, there is not a more secure, rewarding position in business. You experience tremendous freedom, significant financial rewards, and deep, satisfying relationships with your clients.

If you are in the revenue-producing side of an organization—in sales, business development, or account management—you want to be a rainmaker, and in this book Kelly Riggs will show you how. It won't be easy. It will take patience, discipline, mental toughness, and skill, but if you possess the first three of those qualities, *Quit Whining and Start SELLING!* will take care of the last.

I found this book to be a comprehensive sales tool. It clearly defines the attitude and the perseverance a top salesperson needs to have; it provides a clear process for achieving success; and it offers tremendous motivation for making this leap. Kelly, as always, interjects real life stories into the text so that it is both meaningful and entertaining. As I read it, I found myself wishing I had read it years ago when I started my career.

Quit Whining and Start SELLING! is an excellent book because it is written by an excellent leader. Kelly has assisted me and my companies in a variety of ways, including sales training, executive coaching, strategic planning, and motivational speaking. He is a perennial favorite as a trainer and keynote speaker because he, like this book, is engaging, hard-hitting, and practical.

Most importantly, Kelly practices what he preaches. After a very successful career in sales and sales management, Kelly formed a consulting company, Vmax Performance Group. He has experienced the challenges of selling, leading a sales team, and owning his own business, and he has been highly successful in every role. Most importantly, he has simultaneously maintained a wonderful marriage, family, and spiritual life.

I believe it's always important to take advice from those who have excelled in the area in which you choose to excel. I encourage you to use this book to create the future you have always dreamed of.

— **Sean Kouplen**, CEO, Regent Bank, successful entrepreneur, and author of the best seller, *Out of the Blocks: A Student's Journey to a Fulfilling Career and Life*

"The only thing worse than training your salespeople and having them leave is not training them and having them stay."
— *Zig Ziglar*

"Selling doesn't exactly have a stellar reputation."
— *Daniel Pink*

EVERYBODY SELLS. Most people will never admit it, but let's face it, everybody is selling something. An idea. An evening out. A choice. A change. Something. Call it something else if it makes you more comfortable—persuasion, influence, whatever—but it is what it is. Everybody sells. That's life.

The same is true in business. You can easily make the argument that everyone in a company is a salesperson of sorts. There may be an official Sales Representative whose job it is to identify and acquire customers, but employees in every department in the company—accounting, operations, manufacturing, administration, and so on—may potentially influence the customer *not* to buy. Or to continue buying, depending on the experience a customer may have with them.

Officially speaking, U.S. labor statistics say that one in every nine workers in America is in the profession of sales. That is more than 15 million Americans who earn their living directly from the sales profession, but that's only the official number. In his book, *To Sell is Human: The Surprising Truth About Moving Others*, author Daniel Pink points out that there are vast numbers of workers spending considerable parts of their workday, as he says, "selling in a broader sense—persuading, influencing, and convincing others." The current economy, influenced significantly by a wave of technological innovation, has produced an avalanche of "artisans, non-employer businesses, free agents, [and] micro-entrepreneurs" who are, says Pink, (gasp!) "selling all the time."

From Pink's point of view, this "new" generation of sellers is breaking the mold on the traditional notion we have of salespeople. The perfect example is Cannon-Brookes, a software company that tallied $100 million in revenue last year without employing a single "traditional" salesperson:

> But the employees who offer support, unlike a traditional sales force, don't tempt callers with fast-expiring discounts or badger them to make a long-term commitment. Instead, they simply help people understand the software, knowing that the value and elegance of their assistance can move wavering buyers to make a purchase. The same goes for engineers. Their job, of course, is to build great software—but that demands more than just slinging code. It also requires discovering customers' needs, understanding how the products are used, and building something so unique and exciting that someone will be moved to buy.

This is the alleged "new" face of selling. Employees of Cannon-Brookes don't really sell in the sense that one would perceive as the role of a traditional salesperson. Certainly, they don't stoop to "tempting" or "badgering" customers. Instead, they simply help those customers understand how Cannon-Brookes' products and services can best serve their specific needs.

And therein lies the problem.

The common perception of selling and salespeople is a caricature that has been created and fostered by bad salespeople, popular film (think *Tin Men* or *Glengarry, Glen Ross*), and the omnipresent telephone solicitor. The portrait of a pushy, obnoxious, fast-talking self-promoter who uses every kind of questionable tactic to separate people from their money is more than common, and it is the worst possible billboard for the profession.

But the reality is that great salespeople can be found all over the country working with thousands of companies that depend upon them to help their businesses succeed. And—surprise, surprise—those professionals have been selling like the people at Cannon-Brookes for a very long time.

The truth is that the profession of selling isn't inherently bad. Unfortunately, the way in which some industries have gone about the task of selling has helped sustain the negative opinions of the profession. The disapproval is understandable, of course. Bad salespeople abound and the great ones are rarely, if ever, in the news or on the big screen.

For these reasons, selling is still considered a sketchy career choice. 15 million salespeople in the country and, sadly, a significant percentage of those salespeople continue to contribute to the negative stereotype attached to the profession. Only a fraction are truly successful professionals. Most are just mediocre.

Which implies a tremendous opportunity.

INTRODUCING 1-ON-1 SELLING™

Throughout his career, legendary sales trainer and motivational speaker Zig Ziglar said that customers buy from those salespeople they like and trust. In other words, people buy from people, and 'people' is you, the salesperson. From the customer's perspective, you are the one who made the case for change. You are the one who promised, implicitly or explicitly, to deliver. You are the one that customers expect to resolve any problems they experience because the customer trusts you.

That is the essence of 1-on-1 Selling™, a consultative relationship between a customer and a salesperson.

1-on-1 Selling™ is a compilation of the ideas and concepts I have learned and developed over the course of three decades of selling—as a salesperson, sales manager, sales trainer, and, most importantly, as a business owner. Some of these ideas were adapted from influential sales managers; some came from the hundreds of books and articles I have devoured over the years; and more than a little bit of what you will read here is the result of a whole lot of mistakes that I have made that have cost me a lot of money over the years.

It's not that there is any lack of books on selling; quite the contrary. There is an overwhelming abundance of books available to the ambitious sales professional. A scan of bookstore titles would suggest that you can learn how to close sales, manage complex sales, and negotiate sales. You can learn how to sell solutions, become a rainmaker, or become a heavy hitter. According to one title, you can learn how to sell anything to anybody. There's conceptual selling, strategic selling, spin selling, niche selling, zero-resistance selling, and how-to-master-the-art-of selling.

Many of these books are "must reads" for anyone who cares to become a professional salesperson, and most of them reside in my own library. However, I decided to write this book in order to create a single work that explores a number of mission-critical sales topics, some of which are not typically addressed in other sales guides: competitive advantages, the sales process, defending margins, territory management, strategic sales planning, and a host of other specific skills that will allow you to dramatically improve your skills.

Just in case you're not satisfied with mediocrity.

PART I

GETTING STARTED

CHAPTER 1

THE OPPORTUNITY OF A LIFETIME

"The man who can drive himself further once the effort gets painful is the man who will win."
— **Roger Bannister**

"Keep away from people who try to belittle your ambitions. Small people do that, but the really great make you feel that you, too, can become great."
— **Mark Twain**

ON ANY NUMBER OF LEVELS, selling is an immensely rewarding profession. In fact, if you had to choose a single word to capture the essence of the profession, it would have to be 'opportunity.'

Selling provides those with an entrepreneurial spirit the opportunity to pursue their dreams, often with very little risk. It provides the opportunity for an individual to create an income far beyond what might normally be possible in other circumstances. It provides the opportunity for those motivated by achievement or competition to find an outlet to fulfill those needs. For those who seek to work independently, it provides the opportunity to be judged on one's own merits.

The story of Chris Gardner (*The Pursuit of Happyness*) provides a vivid illustration of what is possible in the sales profession. In the early 80s, Gardner's life was a train wreck. His venture into the medical sales profession had been a bust and his personal life was in the same downward plunge as his career. A nasty verbal confrontation with his girlfriend (and the mother of his one-year old son) brought the police around. They quickly determined that Gardner, if nothing else, had $1,200 in outstanding parking tickets, extra little gifts he had earned while desperately searching for a job.

With no job and no money, he was unable to pay the fines, an insurmountable hurdle that landed him in jail for ten days. Locked up in a cage, with the specter of additional charges looming over his head like vultures over a dead carcass, Gardner had ten long days to dwell on his past—the bad decisions, the poor judgment, the critical missteps.

Unfortunately, his release from jail didn't change his perspective. His girlfriend hadn't pressed charges, but now it was just goodbye and no thanks—a farewell that provided him with even more bad news. Although she had awarded him sole custody of their son, the boarding house he temporarily called home was firmly enforcing their no-kids-allowed policy. He and Chris, Jr. would have to find another place to live—immediately—and their prospects were less than stellar.

Gardner was now a homeless, single father living on the streets of San Francisco with a toddler. With little more to his name than the clothes on his back, he was living one day at a time, searching for places to sleep and scrounging for enough money to survive.

Gardner's childhood memories certainly offered no inspiration. He had grown up poor and never knew his biological father. His stepfather had been an abusive alcoholic. His mother had gone to prison. He had spent time in foster care. Life had been one bitter failure after another. But things were about to change.

The spark that would ignite the rest of his life arrived in the nick of time—in a spectacular red Ferrari.

THE COURAGE TO CONTINUE

It was Winston Churchill who declared, "Success is not final; failure is not fatal. It is the courage to continue that counts." In the final analysis, there is nothing like failure, or hardship, or an ultimatum to reveal whether any individual—especially a salesperson—is willing to invest what it takes to separate from the rest of the pack; to determine if one is willing to persevere in the face of rejection; to overcome obstacles and circumstances and create one's own success.

Chris Gardner, as it turns out, was one of those individuals. More than anything in the world, he wanted to discover what profession would allow someone to own that gorgeous Ferrari. That car, and the impeccably dressed man sitting behind the wheel, represented the success that Gardner could only dream about.

Dialing up his courage, he introduced himself to the driver and wasted no time asking him what he did for a living. The man, he learned, was a stockbroker, a revelation that would completely change Gardner's life. Whatever the sacrifice, whatever the cost, he decided he would do anything necessary to become a stockbroker. Despite his previous failure in sales, despite his current circumstances, despite his hardships, and despite his background, he would find a way.

Gardner eventually secured a job interview with Dean Witter Reynolds and was, almost miraculously, accepted for an internship position with the company. Once on board, his immediate objective was ridiculously simple; he would simply outwork everyone in the office. His daily goal was two hundred prospecting phone calls, every single day. At night, with his son safely asleep, he would study for his brokerage license—often in a homeless shelter, occasionally in the subway bathroom, wherever he and Chris Jr. happened to be that night.

Having glimpsed a way out of his plight, Gardner was unwilling to allow anything to deter him. He had experienced a point in life that most cannot imagine and very few are forced to endure, but he would not give up. He would not be victimized. He would not blame others.

Failure was not a word to even consider.

IF IT WAS EASY, ANYONE COULD DO IT

No one ever said success was easy, just that it is possible. If you look hard enough, even those individuals that seem to make it look easy have a story to tell—of working long hours after others have given up, of spending time learning what others won't, of practicing critical skills when others choose to simply wing it.

And so it was with Gardner. His motivation wasn't simply to have a job or to earn a decent salary. His commitment was to something much more powerful—to achieve a level of success that would forever deliver him from a life of poverty, to a standard of living that would allow him to provide security and stability for his son.

That burning desire created a work ethic that rapidly paid dividends. In short order, he earned a reputation at Dean Witter Reynolds as a broker who could find and attract new customers. It wasn't long before his success attracted the attention of someone else, an executive at Bear Stearns who offered Gardner the chance to jump into the fast lane. With an opportunity to substantially increase his base salary, Gardner was able to leave his life on the streets forever.

As he continued to learn and grow in the financial services industry, he was also presented with additional opportunities. Eventually, in 1987, just five years after joining Dean Witter Reynolds at a monthly salary of $1,000, Gardner founded his own firm in Chicago—Gardner Rich & Co.—which he continues to lead today.

As a salesperson, I know you have a dream—of personal success, bigger paychecks, recognition, advancement, and promotion. The question is, are you willing to do what it takes to make that dream a reality? Are you willing to invest in your future? To put in the hours and the effort necessary to take your career to the next level?

Do you have the desire and discipline to seize the opportunity of a lifetime?

1-on-1 Principle™
Success in selling will come in direct proportion to your willingness to confront and overcome the obstacles you encounter in your career.

CHAPTER 2

THE VALUE OF FIVE MORE HITS

"It is time for us to stand and cheer for the doer, the achiever, the one who recognizes the challenge and does something about it."

— *Vince Lombardi*

"A man has to have goals—for a day, for a lifetime—and that was mine, to have people say, 'There goes Ted Williams, the greatest hitter who ever lived.'"

— *Ted Williams*

TED WILLIAMS WON BASEBALL'S coveted Triple Crown twice in his career, and came (literally) within an eyelash of winning it twice more. To give you an idea of the immensity of that accomplishment, consider that only 13 players in Major League Baseball history have ever won the Triple Crown. Only one other player, Rogers Hornsby, has ever won it twice.*

Considered by many to be the greatest hitter in the history of baseball, Williams was also the last player in the major leagues to hit over .400, but the core of his greatness wasn't superior talent—it was superior focus. One sportswriter observed that Ted Williams "studied hitting as if he had been assigned to the Manhattan Project."

> Nothing about either hitting or pitching escaped him, and nothing was deemed too trivial. He studied pitchers. He studied umpires. He studied wind patterns. He was even credited with pioneering the use of rosin, mixing the powder with olive oil to make a sticky substance that pre-dated pine tar by about 10 years.

Williams prepared for every at-bat as if it were the most important at-bat in his career. It was that discipline to plan and prepare that enabled him to finish his career with baseball's seventh highest batting average (.344), the all-time best for players with over 500 career home runs.

In most any sport, the difference between average and extraordinary is actually surprisingly small. Major League Baseball is a great example. In the big leagues, the difference between an average major league player and a player headed to the Hall of Fame is only five hits.

Think about it. A player whose career batting average is .250—25 hits for every 100 at-bats—is a respectable major league baseball player. On the other hand, a player who hits .300 in his career—30 hits for every 100 at-bats—will be recognized with a bronze bust in Cooperstown.

Five more hits in every one hundred at-bats.

Looked at from this perspective, greatness doesn't seem so elusive, but make no mistake; those five additional hits can be very difficult. Almost 18,000 players have played Major League Baseball. As of January 2012, only 297 had been inducted into the Hall of Fame—less than two percent of all players.

What is the equivalent of five more hits in selling? Well, if you currently close four deals out of ten, what would one more deal—closing five out of ten opportunities—do for your numbers? The math says you would increase your sales revenue by an average of 25 percent, just by closing one more deal out of ten. However—and this is a concept you will learn in *Quit Whining and Start SELLING!*—if that one additional deal each month creates as much revenue as one of your top accounts, you could easily increase sales by 50 percent!

Study selling like Ted Williams studied hitting and you will not only steadily increase your batting average, you will rapidly make your way to the top two percent of your profession.

> **1-on-1 Principle™**
> Great salespeople don't become great by accident.

*In September 2012, after I had written this chapter, the Detroit Tiger's Miguel Cabrera became the 14th Major League Baseball player to capture baseball's Triple Crown—the first since Carl Yastrzemski last accomplished the feat in 1967.

CHAPTER 3

LOSE THE WHINING

"Nothing is impossible; there are ways that lead to everything, and if we had sufficient will we should always have sufficient means. It is often merely for an excuse that we say things are impossible."
— Francois De La Rochefoucauld

"Ninety-nine percent of the failures come from people who have the habit of making excuses."
— George Washington Carver

NOT LONG AGO I had the opportunity to speak at a two-day business conference that also featured a keynote presentation from Danny Cahill. In case you don't keep up with reality show headlines, Danny participated in Season 8 of *The Biggest Loser*.

Actually, he did more than participate. He won. And, in winning, he became the show's *Biggest Loser Ever*.

When Danny first appeared at the *Biggest Loser* ranch in 2009, he tipped the scales at a whopping 430 pounds. Unless you've been there personally, I seriously doubt you can imagine the physical and emotional suffering that accompanies that kind of body weight. The world looks and feels completely different when the simple things in life are no longer simple.

But, after seven grueling months, Danny weighed in for the final time. The numbers bounced around for a few seconds and finally settled on 191 pounds! Danny had lost an astounding 239 pounds, over 55 percent of his original body weight.

To gain some perspective on the magnitude of what he had accomplished, recognize that the average 6-foot tall American male weighs approximately 180 to 190 pounds. That is almost exactly where Danny wound up, but he had to lose the equivalent of himself *plus* another 40 pounds to get there! He had become, quite literally, less than half the man he used to be.

And he had become the *Biggest Loser Ever.*

Danny's story is incredibly inspiring. The "before" and "after" pictures are jaw dropping. But Danny is one-in-a-million. Maybe ten million. Finding a way to lose over half of your weight? Most people would be happy to take off the 10 to 20 pounds they picked up over the holidays.

But, Danny's experiences in losing weight prior to appearing on *The Biggest Loser* are similar to most other people. He had tried losing weight before. Again and again. The problem, he says, is at 400 pounds you can lose 60 pounds and never really tell the difference. After weeks of struggle and sacrifice, you look in the mirror and you still look the same. It's too easy—*way* too easy—to get discouraged and simply give up.

To just quit.

That, says Danny, was the real problem. Time after time, he quit. And every single time, he regained those 60 pounds. To win *The Biggest Loser* contest, he would have to find a way to break through that built-in excuse. To live life at a normal weight, he would have to find the motivation to do more than just lose weight.

He had to find a way to lose his "quit."*

THE BAD ECONOMY AND OTHER BAD EXCUSES

For most people, quitting is easy. Especially when there is something or someone else to blame. And, by the way, have you ever noticed there is always a something or a someone else around?

Over the course of my career, I think I've heard most of the excuses salespeople have dreamed up to explain their lack of success:

- Our marketing is bad.

- Our product needs work.

- My territory isn't any good.

- I don't get good leads.

- Our prices are too high.

- My quota is unreasonable.

- The economy is struggling.

- People aren't spending money.

The sad truth is, when things aren't going well, it's very easy to blame circumstances. The vast majority of the time, however, the only person to blame is you. Sales success is not easy, but it isn't the product of luck any more than failure is the product of circumstance.

Learn that lesson right now and you have a much better chance of creating a Hall of Fame sales career.

The only thing that is going to get between you and a successful sales career is your willingness, or unwillingness, to blame something or someone else for your performance. Trust me; there will be plenty to blame if you want to. There are no perfect companies. There are no perfect territories. There are no perfect products. Much less all three.

Don't get the wrong idea. I'm not suggesting that being successful in selling will be easy. It will be a lot of hard work.

But it won't be nearly as hard as losing 239 pounds.

Guaranteed.

> **1-on-1 Principle**™
> Save the excuses. Victims make terrible salespeople.

*Note: For more information about Danny Cahill, and to purchase his book, *Lose Your Quit: Achieving Success One Step at a Time*, visit his personal website at www.thedannycahill.com.

CHAPTER 4

THE FIRST THREE STEPS OF YOUR JOURNEY

"If you have the desire to excel, the discipline required for the hours of practice and hard work will come more easily. There are no overnight successes. It takes time, work and patience."

— *George Burns*

"You are never too old to set another goal or dream a new dream."

— *C. S. Lewis*

SO, YOU'RE A SALESPERSON. Maybe you're just getting started, or maybe you're a veteran. Maybe you're frustrated with your progress, or maybe you're just looking for an edge over your competition. You might even be wondering if you have what it takes to succeed in selling. Regardless of your motives, you are apparently looking to move your career and income forward or you probably wouldn't be reading this book.

Let's start with a question: How does your day start?

Do you wake up each morning dreading the day and struggling to get moving? Do you look for reasons to procrastinate? Does fear overwhelm you? If so, you are either working for the wrong company, stuck in victim mode blaming something or somebody else for your failures, or you're in the wrong profession altogether. No matter what the cause, you first need to make a decision.

Are you willing to take responsibility for your own success, or will you continue to blame your circumstances?

On the other hand, if you wake up each morning with genuine anticipation, wondering how you can increase your income, get the next sale, or defeat a competitor, you very likely have exactly what it takes to reach the top two percent of your profession. If you hate to lose, and you're willing to learn and practice the habits of top sales-people, there is very little that can stop you.

This is critical: You are not destined to fail. Nor are you destined to succeed. You are simply destined to whatever you have the desire and discipline to create. And you always have the freedom, and the opportunity, to make a new choice and create a new set of circum-stances.

So, if you're prepared to get serious about your success, let's get moving. The first three steps of your journey are simple:

1. Write down your dreams.

What do you really want to accomplish this year, and over the next three years? How much money do you really want to make? What short-term goals must you set to fulfill your dreams? Write them all down.

Write. Them. Down.

No excuses, just write them down. Take as long as you need to, but get your dreams on paper. To be successful, you need a very clear picture of what that success looks like.

Then, you want to discuss them with someone who truly cares about your success. Why? Because you need someone to encourage you. You need—desperately need—to be accountable to someone.

The very best thing that happened to me early in my sales ca-reer was the day my wife found out my company offered a two-week, all-expenses-paid trip to Hawaii for any salesperson who reached the top level of the prestigious President's Club. After that, I never needed a sales manager—I had one living in the same house.

To go to Hawaii meant that I would need to accomplish something no salesperson in the company had achieved previous-ly, and it would require an increase in my sales revenue of more than 40 percent in a single year. But I learned how powerful it is to have a clear target to shoot for and an intense motivation to hit it. One year later, I booked our trip to Maui.

Write down your dreams. Share them with someone. Never lose sight of them.

2. Resolve to master your company's products and/or services.

As we will discover, customers want to do business with salespeople who can provide solutions, develop new ideas, and solve their problems. To be that salesperson, you must learn everything you can about your products and/or services and their applications.

You never know when a single product benefit, technical specification, or specialized application may be the single difference in allowing you to develop a winning idea and capture a sale. So, you need to absorb everything you can about your products and services and their applications within the next six months—not just the information in the brochure or catalog, but the behind-the-scenes stuff that marks an expert.

Who in the company can help you? Who can teach you what you need to know to become a recognized expert?

When I traveled to the corporate office, I spent as much time as I could with the engineers and the research team. I spent time on the manufacturing floor so that I could observe fabrication and assembly processes. I spent time with the customer service department so that I could learn how the company resolved common customer issues. The knowledge gained during those visits paid enormous dividends.

The key here is that in-depth knowledge, used appropriately, builds lasting credibility with customers. There is a significant difference between a product salesperson and a product expert. The first knows the product; the second *understands* the product.

Don't wait. Do it right now. Create a detailed plan to develop a master's understanding of your products.

3. Resolve to master your industry.

The next logical extension of becoming recognized as an expert is to master the industry that you work in. When customers come to rely on you as a source of information, and new applications, and best practices within your industry, you will become much more than a salesperson. You will become acknowledged as a consultant.

As you did in step two, create a plan to dramatically increase your industry knowledge over the next 6 to 12 months. What trade publications or periodicals can you read? Who in the industry can serve as your mentor? Where can you go to learn what you need to know in order to be viewed as an industry expert? Does your company or industry offer certifications or other training that you need?

Your objective is to rapidly achieve "consultant" status with your customers. For some industries, that learning curve is a long one; for others, the ramp-up can happen very quickly.

How long will it take for you to become the industry expert you need to be?

While there is much more to achieving greatness in selling than mastering your industry and absorbing everything you can about your company's products and services, you will never reach your potential until you do. Customers have made that clear.

In a comprehensive 2007 survey conducted by H.R. Chally Group, customers clearly stated that they want salespeople who understand their businesses, can diagnose and solve their problems, and are able to design the appropriate application or solution for their specific challenges.

In other words, they demand that you become a skilled professional. Not a glib, fast-talking, back-slapping, joke-telling, doughnut-delivering sales pretender.

> **1-on-1 Principle™**
> High-performance salespeople are consultants who are viewed as experts.

1-on-1 Principles™

Chapter 1:
Success in selling will come in direct proportion to your willingness to confront and overcome the obstacles you encounter in your career.

Chapter 2:
Great salespeople don't become great by accident.

Chapter 3:
Save the excuses. Victims make terrible salespeople.

Chapter 4:
High-performance salespeople are consultants who are viewed as experts.

PART II

WHAT ARE YOU SELLING?

CHAPTER 5

THE BETTER MOUSETRAP THEORY

"If a man has good corn or wood, or boards, or pigs, to sell, or can make better chairs or knives, crucibles or church organs than anybody else, you will find a broad hard-beaten road to his house, though it be in the woods."

— Ralph Waldo Emerson

"If all you're trying to do is essentially the same thing as your rivals, then it's unlikely that you'll be very successful."

— Michael Porter

SEVERAL YEARS AGO I went to work for a start-up company that had developed a revolutionary new product in the hearing industry. From a sales perspective, it was a dream opportunity. The product was unique and easily differentiated from the competition, but, most importantly, it had that "wow" factor; when patients tried it for the first time, that was usually the first word out of their mouths.

Imagine someone whose hearing has begun to falter—the words they miss, the conversations they don't hear. At first it's just frustrating, but over time, hearing loss leads to social isolation and a compromised quality of life.

Then imagine that hearing loss being restored. Not just the ability to hear words again, but the ability to hear the full spectrum of sound. Harmony. Nuance. Like adding color to a black-and-white photograph. Like listening to a scratchy, incomplete AM radio signal and suddenly switching over to a full, dynamic stereo sound reproduction on the FM dial.

The sound quality of this product was nothing short of amazing.

You would think the product would sell itself. Unfortunately, the reality of selling is that a better mousetrap doesn't necessarily ensure a sale. This, of course, is exactly why you need salespeople—to overcome obstacles.

Over lunch one day, the company's owners and I were discussing sales strategy. Actually, I was mostly listening. The owners were expressing their, uh…concern. Despite excellent revenue growth, they were quite troubled that sales weren't increasing as quickly as they thought they should. They reminded me over and over again that we sold the very best product in the industry.

They thought customers should be lining up to give us their money and they wanted to know what we were doing wrong.

Actually, they wanted to know what the National Sales Manager was doing wrong. That was me. And they wanted to know what the salespeople were doing wrong, as I was responsible for them. They wanted to know if we were making enough calls. They wanted to know *how many* calls we were making. Their logic was pretty straightforward—more calls equals more sales. We obviously weren't working hard enough.

Midway through the conversation I stopped them and asked what they thought we were selling to our customers. I wanted to know how they would answer the customer's question, "Why should I buy from you?" I hoped to demonstrate that a number of factors weigh into a customer's buying decision, factors that included much more than just the product itself. Factors that needed to be addressed and had nothing to do with the number of calls we were making.

One of the two owners answered immediately. "That's easy," he said. "We have the finest product on the market and every single patient will benefit from using it." I acknowledged my complete agreement, but I persisted: "Be more specific. As a company, what exactly are we trying to sell to our customers? What is our competitive advantage in the marketplace?"

He gave me that 'Are-you-really-that-dense?' look; the one you get when you've crossed over from mildly annoying to unreasonably senseless. "Our product," he said with pronounced emphasis, "is better than anything out there. That's what we're selling."

"Here is the challenge," I responded. "There are at least a dozen other companies out there saying exactly the same thing, and every single one of those companies has a marketing budget far greater than ours. Their message is far louder than ours and they have far more credibility in the marketplace. Customers aren't going to throw their doors open to us and completely change their business practices just because we claim we have the best product in the marketplace."

And they didn't. Despite two years of excellent growth, the company didn't come close to reaching its sales potential. Why? Because our customers wanted more than the claim of a superior product. They wanted the support that other vendors were willing to provide but the owners were unwilling to concede. They wanted to bypass some of the company's policies that made it difficult for them to do business with us. And, most importantly, they needed help in making the adjustment to a completely different style of hearing instrument.

The owners, very bright and capable men, never seemed to come to terms with the fact that customers don't simply make buying decisions based on product performance. Even when a company enjoys a distinct product advantage—which we most definitely did—it still has to gain traction with the customer. Credibility has to be established and the customer's trust has to be earned.

In other words, customers need a very good reason to change years of buying habits, especially if you're asking them to move away from something that is already working. Customers will often forego a superior solution for that reason alone—because the change itself represents too much of a challenge. Change can be difficult and is often quite costly—transitioning inventory, reconfiguring business processes, retraining employees, and so on. Unfortunately, we were brand new in the industry and, for the most part, unknown and untested. We had to negotiate our way past a number of hurdles that had absolutely nothing to do with the performance of the product.

The lesson here is simple: there are many reasons for changing products or vendors, but there are plenty of reasons for not making a change. A better mousetrap simply does not ensure that customers will beat a path to your door (with all due respect to Ralph Waldo Emerson).

1-on-1 Principle™
Customers need compelling reasons to make a change. A great product is critical, but it is often not enough.

CHAPTER 6

"Why Should I Buy From You?"

"I find it useful to remember, everyone lives by selling something."
— *Robert Louis Stevenson*

"If you stay in the shadow of your larger competitors and never establish your 'differentness', you will always be weak."
— *Jack Trout*

"WHY SHOULD I BUY FROM YOU?" Customers may come right out and ask you that question, or they may not, but make no mistake, the question is implied. In your initial meeting, the customer flips over an imaginary five-minute sand timer and the silent dialogue begins:

> Give me a reason to listen.
>
> Give me a reason to invest my valuable time in further conversation.
>
> Give me a reason to consider you as a solution.

If time runs out and you haven't captured the customer's imagination, the window on that opportunity slams shut. It is the answer to this one question that is critical in allowing you to gain shelf space in your customer's mind.

Explaining to a customer why they should buy from you is the process of differentiating you and your company in the mind of the customer. It is absolutely critical to your success in selling. Joan Magretta, author of *Understanding Michael Porter: The Essential Guide to Competition and Strategy*, explains:

The key to competitive success—for businesses and nonprofits alike—lies in an organization's ability to create unique value. Porter's prescription: aim to be unique, not best. Creating value, not beating rivals, is at the heart of competition.

Rephrased: If you want to compete successfully, you have to create value in the mind of your customer. Look or sound like everyone else and you are doomed to failure. That being said, it should be self-evident that your primary objective is to understand what you are *really* selling.

What is it that will compel customers to do business with you?

How Do You Compete with UPS?

Rick Jones is the CEO of Lone Star Overnight, a regional player in the logistics industry. Jones assumed leadership of the company in 2010 after three years as the chief operating officer, and his mission was very simple—return the company to profitability.

There was, however, a minor hurdle to contend with. Well, actually, there were two hurdles: UPS and FedEx. Not exactly the easiest problem to solve on the first day. How do you compete with not one, but two 500-pound gorillas? After all, playground bullies have the capacity to bully for a reason. They are bigger and badder than all the other kids.

But Jones had some insight into a possible solution. The answer, he believed, was to create a niche in the market, to discover an issue or a problem that a smaller, more flexible company like Lone Star Overnight could solve, and, in doing so, create a competitive advantage. He found the answer by doing something simple—he talked to his customers.

Mr. Jones, who spent his formative years in management at U.P.S., looked closely at customer feedback and had an aha moment when he noticed a pattern in the compliments his company received. Lone Star's small-to-medium-sized business customers appreciated responsiveness, a willingness to accept responsibility for actions and fix problems quickly. Customers also liked the flexibility of drivers who were willing to wait for packages or pick up lab samples at 3 a.m. They also said they liked that Lone Star drivers and staff were friendly.

(Mueller, *You're the Boss*, April 26, 2012)

Jones seized that information and set out to differentiate Lone Star Overnight from his bigger rivals. It would require a remodeling of the company's culture, but it would provide the differentiation Lone Star needed. Indeed, it was the company culture that would prove to be the differentiation: Be responsive. Be flexible. Be friendly. Make it a good day for the customer.

Not exactly mind-boggling, but that is the point. A competitive advantage doesn't have to stem from a revolutionary new product or service, or exist because of the company's size, market share, or history. It might—but it doesn't have to.

Of course, it's one thing to find an answer, but it's a completely different thing to rebuild your company's culture. But he did.

And it worked.

Imagine the choice a salesperson could pose to a potential shipping customer:

"Yes, you can use UPS or FedEx. You know what you get with them—big companies, plenty of resources. However, if you want to work with a company that will respond immediately, on your schedule, and make it a better day for your staff when they arrive, we are a great fit for your company. Take XYZ Company, for example. Like most companies, they used UPS and FedEx, but they needed someone that would pick up packages at midnight. That's our strong suit."

Here's the key: once a clear difference has been created in the mind of the customer, the customer can make a determination if that difference is worth pursuing. Notice that the "difference" is not a comparison of prices. Price will certainly enter the discussion at some point, but not as a direct comparison upon which to make a decision—a necessity in helping you defend your margins.

FINDING YOUR NICHE

So, your first objective is to identify your competitive advantage(s) in the marketplace, a compelling reason for doing business with you. Your competitive advantage is something of value that cannot be obtained elsewhere. Presenting a unique competitive advantage, especially one that specifically addresses a need you discover, is a critical step in giving you the opportunity to win more sales.

To identify your company's competitive advantage, start with the following questions, and then complete the three exercises below:

> What are we known for?
>
> Why do our best customers buy from us?
>
> Are we recognized as an authority in any sector?
>
> What do we do that is uniquely different than our competitors?
>
> Have we been first at something?
>
> What can we do that no one else can do?
>
> What innovations have we provided?
>
> What do we do that is better, faster, or less expensive than everyone else?

EXERCISES

1. **Research your company.**

What have you accomplished that is unique? What benefits can a customer expect from your company that are not readily available elsewhere? What credentials do you have that represent a clear and unique advantage over your competitors? If at all possible, quantify these items (more on this in Chapter 10).

2. Look carefully at your products and services.

What value do your products or services bring to your customers that cannot be readily duplicated by your competitors? Can you quantify how much money can be made or saved by using your products? Do your engineers, designers, technicians, or installers have experience or certifications that others do not have? Do you have a recognized expert in your company that provides capabilities that the competition cannot match?

3. Talk to your best customers.

Ask your customers why they prefer your company and/or products. Find out what they are buying from you and see if you can quantify it: Are you more convenient? How so? Are your service solutions more effective? What impact has it had on their productivity or profitability?

The truth is that differentiation is possible despite your size or market position. Unless your company is treading water until the end comes, you almost certainly have, or can create, one or more competitive advantages.

But let me offer a word of caution: the first thought most companies have about their "advantage" is to buy into the idea that they are "the best" or have better products or do things better than everyone else. If you start down this road, it will almost certainly keep you from finding meaningful competitive advantages, the things that truly matter to your customers.

Look deep into your company's capabilities, its performance history, and its customer base to find one or more distinctions that can genuinely separate your company from the pack. Things like your company's legacy, your work in the community, specialized services or delivery, your service model, recognized technical superiority, the ease of doing business with your company—any or all of these things may potentially create a competitive advantage for you.

> **1-on-1 Principle™**
> A competitive advantage is a direct and compelling answer to the question of why a customer should choose you instead of a competitor.

CHAPTER 7

THE ILLUSION OF GREAT QUALITY AND EXCELLENT SERVICE

"Competing to be the best leads inevitably to a destructive, zero-sum competition that no one can win. As offerings converge, gain for one becomes loss for the other. This is the very essence of "zero sum." I win only if you lose.

— *Joan Magretta*

"Given a choice—and in most industries today buyers have choices—customers rarely tolerate producers that are not focused on their interests."

— *John P. Kotter*

"WHY SHOULD I BUY FROM YOU?" As I mentioned in Chapter 6, your customer may or may not come right out and ask this question, but rest assured, it is a critical concern. And most salespeople blunder when they answer.

Badly.

Here's what I mean: ask any salesperson why you should buy from him and you will get very predictable answers:

"We have great quality products."

"We have the best customer service in the industry."

"We're the best...the leader in the industry...No. 1... blah, blah, blah."

Dress it up any way you want, these are the top three answers in a landslide. I know because I ask. Every time I work with a group of salespeople, I ask, "Why should I buy from you?" I go around the room and get answers. And I get the same answers, over and over:

"Our solutions are technically superior to our competitors."

"We are dedicated to exceeding our customer's expectations."

"We provide the best service available."

Great quality. Top-notch service. Superior solutions. Commitment to excellence. Exceeding customer expectations. Blah, blah, blah.

A few years ago, I had the opportunity to hear Terri Langhans speak. She is the former CEO of a national advertising agency and has over 20 years of experience in marketing. She now serves as an independent marketing consultant and the name of her company is— seriously—Blah Blah Blah, Inc.* She puts her finger right on this critical sales problem in her excellent book, *The 7 Marketing Mistakes Every Business Makes*:

> A lot of people I work with pound their fists and righteously proclaim how different, better, faster, experienced, specialized and/or affordable their products and services are. They think that quality, service and value sets their business apart. A lot of them also think the Statue of Liberty is in New York. Wrong on both counts. Quality, service and value get you in the game; they don't make you unique. And the Statue of Liberty is technically located in New Jersey.

Get the picture? Even if you do have great quality and great service (which some of your customers may be willing to debate), it doesn't do you a bit of good to say so in such a generic way. The reason is simple—all of your competitors are saying exactly the same thing.

Great quality? Might be true. Doesn't really matter.

Actually, it would matter if you presented the evidence in a compelling way. However, in offering up such generic claims, you have done two things, both of which are bad for you. First, you have sent the message that you are just like your competitors. You sound like them, make the same baseless claims, and generally fail to differentiate yourself in any meaningful way.

Second, because you are no different than your competitors (in the customer's perception), you have created the best possible scenario for the customer: they get to choose from three (or more) acceptable vendors who will all provide exactly what they need. The only thing left to negotiate is price.

Congratulations. You get to give away margin in order to win a deal.

WHAT IS YOUR CUSTOMER BUYING?

The fault lies generally with the way companies train their salespeople. The vast majority of corporate sales training revolves around product knowledge, technical training, and administrative procedures—processing orders, filing expense reports, replenishing marketing materials, things like that. Sure, understanding the features of your product, learning how to demonstrate the product, and absorbing all the details of how to deliver, implement, and install the product is important, but most corporate training stops just short of adequately preparing a salesperson to truly compete.

True, the product training you receive will allow you to explain the actual product or service, and it is likely that your product or services provide some differentiation that may create some distance from your competitors. However, customers are rarely buying just a product or service. They are also buying:

- A business relationship
- Availability
- Delivery
- Implementation
- Training
- Service and support
- Financial terms

Perhaps, most importantly, they are buying a sufficient reason to make a change; in some cases, a considerable change. Buyers risk criticism, embarrassment, and potential loss by making a change in products. So, in a sea of competitors, the most important question to answer is, why should a customer buy from you?

The truth is, the vast majority of companies fail miserably in preparing a salesperson to answer that one very simple question. There are plenty of companies selling the products or services you are selling, so why should a customer buy from you? Why should the customer change?

But wait! You told your customer how much better your product was and showed your customer all the great features they get from you that they can't get from your competitor's product, right? Sorry. Although product differentiation may occasionally win you a sale, the reality is that your 'my-feature-is-better-than-your-feature' sales presentation simply reinforces the notion that you are not any different than your competitor. Your competitors typically do exactly the same thing, scoring points with the product features YOU don't have.

The result? Your customer gets to decide how much to pay for which features. When the customer finally decides which product they want, they simply use the competitors' prices to negotiate a better deal. After all, each of you has great quality, top-notch service, and is dedicated to exceeding their expectations.

So, let's try again. Why should I buy from you?

> **1-on-1 Principle™**
> Customers expect excellent quality and customer service, so generic claims about either of these do nothing to distinguish you from your competitors.

*For more information about Terri Langhans, Certified Speaking Professional and Chief of Everything at Blah Blah Blah, visit http://www.blahblahblah.us.

WHO IS SELLING WHOM?

"Any change, even a change for the better, is always accompanied by drawbacks and discomforts."
— *Arnold Bennett*

"For the seller, selling based on price is like heroin. The short-term gain is fantastic, but the more you do it, the harder it becomes to kick the habit."
— *Simon Sinek*

SOME YEARS AGO, I managed a number of very capable and talented inside sales professionals in a start-up venture. One salesperson, in particular, was very good. He had an easygoing manner about him and customers really enjoyed hearing from him. He was thorough, professional, and responsive. His only downfall was that his customers were often better at selling *him* than he was at selling them.

Day after day, potential customers overwhelmed him with price objections, and with enough time he began to empathize with their plight. Business was tough, they said. It's tough to compete, they said. You just don't understand, they said—to use your products, we simply MUST get a lower price.

And he believed them.

Don't get me wrong—I know how tough it is out there. I know you get beat up every single day on price. After months of that, you tend to forget that customers need many of the things you offer, but you may not have figured out how to create value for those things. In the meantime, your customer turns out to be a better salesperson than you.

With little understanding of the complexities of creating real value for the prospect, lazy salespeople quickly discover that, to win a sale, the only significant negotiation tool they have is the ability to give away the company's money—in other words, to lower prices.

Why? Because a prospect will have little interest in paying a premium price for an undifferentiated product that appears to be nothing more or less than what a competitor is offering.

That is great news for your prospects, by the way. If all the solutions are similar, all they have to do is create a bidding war and wait for the lower price to emerge.

Of course, this problem gets worse—much worse—when the economy goes south. There are fewer opportunities and more people willing to cut prices to get business. Even solid salespeople who should know better can be guilty of giving up and giving in just to win a deal. The reasoning is that a thinner margin is better than no margin.

Which, of course, is to completely miss the point.

Clearly, there are times when a company will make the determination that lowering prices is in the company's best interest, but that should be a strategic decision, not a tactical one made by a desperate salesperson who has completely failed to give the company a chance to get full value.

But, let's get to the bottom line. In most cases, salespeople become convinced they must lower prices. Their excuses are consistent and predictable: The poor economy has created a buyer's market. The competition is lowering prices ("We're not competitive."). Buyers are slashing their budgets. If you are a business owner or a sales manager, you have heard it all before:

"You don't understand. They can get the same product down the street for 20 percent less."

"I didn't have a choice. I had to make a decision. There are three other vendors right behind me willing to make that deal."

"Customers just won't pay our price in this economy. They don't have to."

The truth is, buyers are always looking for a better deal. Every business owner is looking to save a buck, so their initial response is likely to question your price and ask for a discount. Frankly, it is the rare buyer who won't claim your price is too high, or suggest that your competition has a better deal, or ask you to sweeten your offer, even when he has already made up his mind to go ahead with the purchase. The worst part is that most salespeople will lower their prices simply because a prospect claims their prices are too high.

Savvy buyers use the same negotiation tactics in just about every transaction:

> "That is a lot more than I want to spend."

> "You'll have to do better than that."

> "I appreciate it, but I can get that same product for less money."

> "I really like your product—it's just what I'm looking for—but your competitor offered me the same deal for 10% less."

> "You know, if you can take 10% off that price, I can make this happen right now."

But why is this a big surprise? Isn't this exactly what buyers are supposed to do? Aren't buyers going to try to negotiate a better deal?

Pay attention, because this is truly important: in most every sales call, there are usually two sales presentations going on—the one in which you are selling a solution and a second one in which the buyer is selling you on lowering your price.

The question is, who is selling whom?

1-on-1 Principle™

In most transactions the prospect is selling just as hard as you—for lower prices, better terms of sale, and several other considerations.

CHAPTER 9

THE PROBLEM WITH 'LOWEST PRICE'

"There is hardly anything in the world that someone cannot make a little worse and sell a little cheaper, and the people who consider price alone are that person's lawful prey."
— *John Ruskin (1819-1900)*

"I don't want to do business with those who don't make a profit, because they can't give the best service."
— *Richard Bach*

COMPANIES HAVE LONG BEEN willing to reduce their prices to remain competitive in the marketplace. Clearly, the easiest possible way to win a sale is to simply give away margin and literally buy the business. Obviously, you can't do that for very long and stay in business, but that minor detail has never prevented companies from venturing off that particular cliff.

In 2009, Office Depot aired a provocative television commercial that illustrates the right approach to this dilemma. In the opening scene of the commercial, a hometown barbershop owner (Dan) watches helplessly as a discount haircutting chain (Nitro Cutz) opens a garish new store right across the street. Hanging in the windows of the newly constructed building are huge signs with a very precise message:

$6 Haircuts.

This, of course, is every small business owner's nightmare—a national chain with superior buying power and a larger marketing budget moving in next door and pricing the local store right out of business. Dan, however, is having none of that. His response? To display a sign of his own detailing his store's competitive, chain-killing advantage:

We Fix $6 Haircuts.

Isn't that brilliant? That simple sign provided the perfect reminder to customers that you get exactly what you pay for. Quality comes at a price, and a lower price usually means sacrificing something important you care about.

Notice that Dan's sign didn't say, "We Provide Better Quality Haircuts," or "Our Service is Worth the Extra $2." Instead, the proprietor created a powerful message to remind customers that price may be important, but it should have some limitations when influencing an important buying decision.*

Which brings me to a critical perspective about the role that price plays in a buying decision. Before you decide that your customers care only about price, consider the following questions:

Does LOWEST PRICE mean the lowest cost to the customer?

Does LOWEST PRICE mean the best final result for the customer?

Does LOWEST PRICE ensure attention to detail?

Does LOWEST PRICE guarantee expertise?

Does LOWEST PRICE mean timely support and follow-up?

Does LOWEST PRICE mean on-time delivery?

Does LOWEST PRICE mean issues will be resolved quickly?

Does LOWEST PRICE mean common sense will be applied to issues?

Does LOWEST PRICE ensure cooperation between multiple vendors?

Does LOWEST PRICE provide opportunity to adapt to new technology?

Does LOWEST PRICE create the best customer experience?

Does LOWEST PRICE mean a full complement of resources can be accessed after the sale?

Does LOWEST PRICE create a standard that ensures clients get what they want?

The point is, in any given buying decision, there are a whole host of factors a customer will consider, and price is only ONE of them. Yet, many salespeople have become convinced that price is the *only* consideration that customers think about. Which, coincidentally, is exactly true, if and when a buyer perceives there is no difference between products. At that point, price does become the primary consideration in the purchase.

This is exactly why differentiation is so critical. If you don't give your customers a compelling reason to consider your company, you literally force yourself into a situation where price must be the determining factor, a situation that cannot end well for you.

I don't want you to misunderstand my point. Customers always care about price. Every single time. Think of yourself as a consumer. Even when you find the exact product or service you want—and no other product will do—you still want the best price possible, right? More than likely you still try to negotiate. But, ideally, a salesperson wants you to negotiate price *after* you have decided that product or service provides something you can't live without or can't get elsewhere.

Customers will try to do just the opposite. Remember, they are selling you just as hard as you are selling them. Their sales pitch is simple: The only thing that will win this particular sale is a lower price. But think about it. What do your customers really want?

The best product.

The best guarantee.

Perfect implementation.

The best customer service.

And the very best price.

In other words, they want it all. They don't really want to compromise in any area; instead, they want the very best of all possible worlds. However, what they need you to believe—what they will tell you over and over again—is that price is the only thing they really do care about.

Why? Because, if they can get you to believe that the deal comes down to the best price, then they absolutely can get it all. The best product. The best service. And, now that you have bought their sales pitch, the best price. All because you failed to give them anything compelling to consider.

If you want to get the price your product deserves, you have to learn to communicate a forceful competitive advantage. You see, when you fail to differentiate your solution, you are actually forcing the customer to negotiate your price.

How is that working out?

1-on-1 Principle™
Your customers want you to believe you are a commodity so that every sales transaction can be about negotiating the lowest price.

---

*In an interesting twist on the Office Depot commercial, the company was forced to withdraw the "$6 Haircut" television spot from its marketing efforts. As it turns out, Jeff Slutsky, author, speaker, and CEO of Street Fighter Marketing, had been presenting that signature story to audiences for years. Coincidentally (wink, wink), not long after Jeff presented the story in a keynote presentation to the National Association of Office Suppliers, it wound up in an Office Depot commercial. The good news is that Office Depot resolved the, uh…issue, to Jeff's satisfaction.

CHAPTER 10

PAINTING BY NUMBERS

"Whether it is a full-blown competitive advantage or simply the table stakes required to enter the game, sales effectiveness will remain a critical ingredient in sale success."
— *Howard Stevens*

"If the only tool you have is a hammer, you tend to see every problem as a nail."
— *Abraham Maslow*

A FEW YEARS AGO, I received a call from a small manufacturing company searching for help with their sales efforts. The company was in a significant bind. Struggling to grow and compete effectively against larger competitors, they had decided to lower prices to attract new customers. Predictably, the results had been nothing short of disastrous.

Although sales increased slightly, profits plummeted. The company's resources were stretched to the breaking point as dwindling profits did not allow for additional investments in people. As might be expected, customer service suffered as customer complaints increased.

This is the classic 'discount–the-product-but-make-it-up-in-volume' sales strategy, also known, coincidentally, as the 'how-to-go-broke-in-a-hurry' strategy. While strategic selling occasionally calls for salespeople to discount prices, indiscriminate price cutting to build volume is a train wreck at best, and a complete company-ending disaster at the worst. Unless your company is perfectly positioned to become the low-cost provider in the industry (the Walmart supply chain strategy), the impact of cutting prices to gain market share is to crush your profits and irreparably damage your brand.

As I began working with the company, the first challenge was to help them understand the value of competitive advantages and how they could be used to strengthen the company's value proposition. Like many companies, they had completely sold out to the idea that price was the only thing their customers really cared about. As a result, they failed to exploit a number of distinct competitive advantages.

For example, one of the company's most valuable, and most profitable, services is to provide a certified rebuild of their primary product line. Customers get a certified, like-new product at a lower price than the original, and the company makes an even better margin than if they were to sell the product new.

Consulting gurus call that a "win-win."

The best part, however, is the company will also rebuild their competitor's product, a service their biggest competitor doesn't offer. Rebuilding the competition's product provides the perfect opening to attract new customers, especially when we learned that customers were frequently commenting that a rebuilt product from my client functioned more reliably than the competitor's new product. And it costs less, as well.

Consulting gurus call that "a tough break for your competitor."

As we dug deeper into the company's operations, we continued to uncover viable competitive advantages. The company provides same-day shipping on a very large inventory of replacement parts, even when ordered late in the day. This is another service unavailable from their primary competitor. As response time can be critical in this particular industry, this advantage allows the company to gain a reputation for superior service at a time when many customers had come to see the larger competitor as slow and difficult to deal with.

Having identified critical advantages that customers would willingly pay for, the company quickly decided to move away from a low-price market strategy and focus on a service differentiation strategy. As a result, the sale of replacement parts and factory rebuilds increased (both carry higher margins), and the positive impact on the bottom line was immediate.

The real lesson in this story, however, is not what the company did, but how they did it. They never touted quality or service to their prospects; instead, they quantified their advantages.

A DEMONSTRATION IS WORTH A THOUSAND WORDS

It's one thing to tell a prospect you have great quality products; it's quite another to prove it. If customers claim your rebuilt products are superior to a competitor's original, it presents a variety of ways to quantify what is obviously a competitive advantage. Think of the following statements as answers to the question, "Why should I buy from you?":

- Because we build reliability into our products. Three out of four customers tell us the quality of our rebuilt product is better than the original they purchased from a competitor.

- Because we care about performance. After letting us rebuild their product, 60 percent of our customers are so impressed with the quality they buy a new product from us as well.

- Because our customers know they can depend on our products. Over half of our new customers say they continue to buy from us because of the performance of our rebuilds.

The point here is that it is very powerful to be able to demonstrate, or prove, your competitive advantages, and the very best way to demonstrate an advantage is to quantify it. Plus, you get double the impact if that proof comes directly from your own customers!

The same idea can be applied to the advantage of having a large inventory of parts that can ship the same day as ordered. "Why should I buy from you?":

- Because we maintain an inventory of over $2 million in parts that we ship the same day if ordered by 4 p.m. One day without a $50 part can cost you hundreds of dollars in down-time.

The truth is, my client discovered they had a great story to tell and the numbers were impressive. In answering the hypothetical question, "Why should I buy from you?" they could communicate "better quality" and "better service" in very real, specific terms.

Not fuzzy, generic claims. Real numbers.

In the commercial construction industry, Flintco is a billion-dollar, third-generation, privately held company headquartered in Tulsa, Oklahoma. In an industry where a typical commercial building project can create any number of difficulties big and small, Flintco boasts an impressive 94 percent customer satisfaction rating. From 2000 to 2010, the company's safety program was recognized five times as one of the top three in the nation. They have received local and national industry awards far too numerous to mention—more than 100 different recognitions of the company's construction excellence.

Flintco's most impressive number, however, may be the percentage of projects awarded to them as the vendor-of-choice. Although most projects in commercial construction are awarded through a standard bidding process, by 2009 the number of Flintco's projects awarded to them directly without a bid process had risen to over 75 percent. Is that something a client would be interested in? Absolutely. It clearly communicates that Flintco has gained a reputation for delivering great value, so much that clients choose the company without asking for competitive bids.

Note that Flintco could claim to have the "best" quality and customer service in the industry, but those words, as we have discovered, would get lost in the clutter of similar claims made by competitors. However, a 94-percent customer satisfaction rating, a top three national safety rating, and more than 100 awards for construction excellence clearly positions Flintco as a firm that customers should consider for their next project.*

And therein lies the point. Wherever possible, you should strive to quantify your competitive advantages. If quality or customer service is truly a differentiated advantage for your company, you must define the advantage with numbers that clearly communicate your edge. Are you faster? Is your turn-around quicker? Do you certify quality in ways that competitors do not? Is your inventory of replacement parts substantially greater than your competitor?

What are the numbers?

A truly differentiated advantage means that competitors, by definition, cannot mimic your numbers. So, in quantifying your advantages, you not only provide a compelling reason to consider your company, you also define the battleground upon which your competitors must try to compete with you.

1-on-1 Principle™
Whenever possible, use numbers to quantify your advantages.

---

*Special thanks to my friend, Dana Birkes, Vice President of Business Development and Marketing at Flintco, for her insight into that great company. As a side note, in January 2013, Flintco was acquired by St. Louis-based Alberici Corporation.

1-on-1 Principles™

Chapter 5:
Customers need compelling reasons to make a change. A great product is critical, but it is often not enough.

Chapter 6:
A competitive advantage is a direct and compelling answer to the question of why a customer should choose you instead of a competitor.

Chapter 7:
Customers expect excellent quality and customer service, so generic claims about either of these do nothing to distinguish you from your competitors.

Chapter 8:
In most transactions the prospect is selling just as hard as you—for lower prices, better terms of sale, and several other considerations.

Chapter 9:
Your customers want you to believe you are a commodity so that every sales transaction can be about negotiating the lowest price.

Chapter 10:
Whenever possible, use numbers to quantify your advantages.

PART III

THE 1-ON-1 SELLING™ PROCESS

CHAPTER 11

THE FOUNDATION OF CONSISTENT SALES PERFORMANCE

"If you can't describe what you are doing as a process, you don't know what you're doing."
— *W. Edwards Deming*

"We overestimate the event and underestimate the process. Every fulfilled dream occurred because of dedication to a process."
— *John Maxwell*

THERE ARE NUMEROUS STORIES of hikers, skiers, and mountain climbers who have trekked off into the wilderness and neglected to prepare themselves for the potential danger of getting lost or disabled in dangerously cold, isolated areas. As we will discover, you can prepare well and do something the right way, or you can simply rush out without thinking.

Chances are you will get two radically different outcomes.

One such story involves 25-year-old Dan Witkowski, who became lost in Washington's North Cascades on December 31, 2003. Witkowski, an avid and extremely capable skier, set out on New Year's Eve to take a few backcountry ski runs and then meet up with some friends for the holiday. The thought of packing survival gear, or worse, getting lost never entered his mind.

[Witkowski] took a chairlift up to a 5,450-foot summit that day, wearing a helmet and the usual gear: gloves, parka and polyester fleece coat, ski pants, a T-shirt and long underwear.

What he didn't have along would turn out to be just as significant: no food, no water, no cell phone, no compass, no emergency equipment. And he hadn't told anyone where he was going or when to expect him back. Worst of all, he broke the unwritten backcountry skier's code when he went outside the designated safe areas. Alone.

On a whim, he decided to take a snowy chute he'd never been down before. When he came to the bottom, he realized he was lost. And the more he tried to find his way back, the more lost he got.

Over the next few days, he climbed ridges, crossed divides and creeks, andtraversed basins, shedding gear as he began to hallucinate. He slept only two hours at a stretch and believed he was walking with the spirits of Native Americans who had once lived there.

At first, no one even knew he was missing.

(Porterfield, *Seattle Times Magazine*, January 9, 2005)

Like most people who become proficient at something they enjoy, Witkowski had developed tremendous confidence in his capabilities. Not only did he ski regularly, he was an experienced "extreme skier" and occasionally worked as a ski instructor. Unfortunately, confidence can lead to a false sense of security, and it did in this case. Witkowski, who opted not to pack survival gear, admitted, "I just didn't like carrying it."

In making that crucial decision, Witkowski neglected to follow a very simple process designed to keep him safe, even in the unlikely event that he skied down the wrong side of a ridge in Snoqualmie Pass—which he did. Those unlikely events, however, are exactly what that process was designed for, and the dangers of neglecting a proven process, no matter how simple, can be catastrophic.

Although he was eventually rescued, Witkowski ultimately lost both legs below the knee to the ravages of frostbite. Despite the tragic outcome, he was fortunate; it could have been far worse. He was discovered five days into his ordeal, just hours before the rescue efforts of 225 people were to be suspended. When found, his core temperature was a mere 85 degrees, and he had shed 20 pounds. Just living to recount the ordeal was described as a miracle.

The lesson here is simple: a process is designed to identify a performance standard and provide a template for training to create and maintain a competence in that performance standard. For anyone who enjoys mountaineering, extreme skiing, or other remote backcountry activities, there is a recommended selection of safety equipment and a number of essential safety precautions designed to keep you alive in the event you become lost or stranded.

If Witkowski had simply adhered to the process—packing necessary survival equipment and following a few simple steps—his misadventure would likely have ended without incident.

THE SALES PROCESS

For many salespeople, the most difficult challenge they will face is the ability to create **consistent sales performance**. Although salespeople will typically succeed to varying degrees because of hard work and good street smarts, *consistent* sales performance can prove elusive without a methodology for identifying the reasons for both success and failure.

Without a sales methodology or process, salespeople experience predictable challenges. While some opportunities are won, others are lost that should have been won. Success often feels random and uncontrollable. Forecasting sales is an exercise in frustration. Salespeople struggle to answer these kinds of questions: What did I do wrong on this opportunity? Why did I lose the sale? Why is my closing ratio so low? Why do I consistently find myself in opportunities that seem to stall or never reach a decision? Why can't I be more consistent in my sales revenue?

For sales managers, this problem is multiplied many times over. A manager's challenge is not only to help an individual salesperson create consistent success, but to create a team of successful salespeople. Making the transition from salesperson to sales manager is tricky simply because the skills required to be a successful salesperson are different than those required to be an effective manager.

In many cases, that frustration will cause a sales manager to micro-manage sales activities and even assume control over larger, more important opportunities to "make sure we don't lose the sale." These sales managers struggle to answer these kinds of questions: Why can't my salespeople hit their numbers? Why does performance vary so much between salespeople who appear to be quite similar? Why does a salesperson who was successful at another company struggle to be successful with us? Why can't I more consistently forecast sales revenue?

When a salesperson doesn't get a sale, where does the problem lie? Is the salesperson's failure due to poor closing skills, the absence of good prospects, a failure to ask good questions, an ineffective presentation, or something else altogether? Is he or she poorly trained or just poorly prepared?

We can guess where the problem lies, but a sales process would likely pinpoint the exact nature of the failure. For instance, if a salesperson is closing two out of ten presentations when five out of ten is the standard, an analysis of the salesperson's performance in comparison to a comprehensive sales process would determine if the problem is in the number or quality of the prospects, the effectiveness of the sales presentations, an inability to resolve the customer's objections, or simply the failure to consistently ask for an order.

But think about some of the advice that is often doled out to salespeople without a clear understanding of the root problem:

"You need to make more calls."

"You need to make more presentations."

"You need to be more enthusiastic."

"You're not asking for the order." (This despite the fact the customer may not have the slightest interest in the product).

"You're just not a salesperson." (Trust me, I heard that one from a manager myself).

On and on it goes; blind stabs in the dark without a clear sense of the real problem. Only in sales does this kind of random advice pass for management feedback.

The result is that salespeople get frustrated at their lack of progress. Worse, when they can't see clearly what needs to be fixed or what skills need to be developed to improve their performance, they often resort to blaming external factors like the economy, their territory, the product line, the company's marketing efforts, or the company's unwillingness to lower prices. More often than not, however, the real issue compromising their sales success is the failure to develop a specific skill, or set of skills, that could be readily identified by a sales process.

But, let's change gears. What if a salesperson is having success in the marketplace? Since salespeople are often successful and do not have a clearly defined sales process, doesn't this negate the need for one? It is a logical question, but the answer is no. The absence of a sales process makes it difficult to know *why* a salesperson is successful.

Is it native talent, blind luck, or sheer doggedness? Does he or she have a special skill or talent that others don't have? Again, sales managers, who desperately want to replicate the success of a particular salesperson are uncertain whether they can teach that success or are forced to rely on hiring born salespeople.

Success in selling certainly requires some native talent, but there are a host of skills that must be developed to capitalize on that talent. Isolating those skills and applying them to a defined sales process enables a sales manager to consistently develop effective salespeople.

1-on-1 Principle™
Implementing an effective sales process is the key to creating consistent sales performance and the only way to truly know what is working and what isn't.

THE RIGHT PLACE AT THE RIGHT TIME

"We are what we repeatedly do. Excellence, then, is not an act,
but a habit."

— *Aristotle*

"Why not just kill them? I'll do it! I'll run up to Paris—bam, bam,
bam, bam. I'm back before week's end. We spend the treasure.
How is this a bad plan?"

— *From the 2002 film, Count of Monte Cristo*

EVERY SALESPERSON BEGINS every single week with exactly the
same amount of time available to everyone else—168 hours. However, that time is perishable, so every single minute you waste is time
you cannot recapture for future use.

The time that you spend chasing down long-shot or low-probability opportunities is time that cannot be recovered. The time
you spend making presentations to people who could never make a
buying decision is time that could have been used to create productive opportunities.

As a salesperson, time is your most precious commodity and you
simply cannot afford to waste it.

What may not be readily apparent is that two equally talented
salespeople may produce dramatically different sales results simply
because one has learned how to maximize his time and the other has
not. While the first salesperson consistently qualifies high-value, high-probability opportunities, the other chases every sales lead equally
and indiscriminately, rushing headlong into a presentation whenever
possible because he believes that "selling is a numbers game."

The truth is that selling is a numbers game, but not in the sense of chasing as many leads as possible or in making as many presentations as possible. Remember the idea about improving your batting average? That is the sense in which selling is a numbers game; a few extra hits every month can be the difference between average and extraordinary.

In order to make the most of your time, you need a defined sales process. One that prevents you from working on the wrong opportunities, talking to the wrong people, addressing the wrong needs, or making an ineffective presentation. One that gets you into the most favorable opportunities, with the best chance to win the sale, while avoiding critical mistakes that could cost you the sale.

A great sales process does all that, and much more. It is simple and easy to remember, yet extremely powerful. Here are the basic steps of the 1-on-1 Selling™ process:

Step 1: Planning
Identify what your "ideal" opportunity looks like.
Blueprint your "ideal" prospects.

Step 2: Discovery
Interview the prospects that fit your plan.
Reveal the prospect's opportunities and current performance gaps.

Step 3: Presentation
Integrate your solution into the customer's unique situation.
Resolve any issues that would prevent you from winning the sale.

Step 4: Delivery
Implement your solution.
Leverage your success.

Plan and discover. Present and deliver. At the macro level, a very simple and easy-to-understand process. Each step, however, is more detailed and has very specific objectives:

> The **planning** phase is designed to prepare for the initial and/or preliminary sales calls and ensure you aren't wasting your time on opportunities that don't make sense. It makes sure you are talking to the right people and know a great deal about the opportunity even before you make your first call.

> The **discovery** phase is oriented around the qualification process and revealing the customer's needs and buying motives. It makes sure you ask the right questions and understand exactly what is important to the customer.

> The **presentation** phase focuses on face-to-face presentation skills, resolution of issues, satisfying the customer's buying criteria, and closing the sale. It makes sure that you match your solution to the customer's needs and create a relationship with the customer that leads inevitably to a win.

> The **delivery** phase is concerned with solution implementation, after-sale follow-up, and the development of additional opportunities. It ensures that you provide exactly what you promised.

Notice that the 1-on-1 Selling™ process begins with a healthy dose of information gathering and opportunity assessment. Again, many salespeople sprint right into the presentation part of selling with little time and effort dedicated to the planning and discovery phases of the process. But, this creates a number of predictable, time-wasting, deal-killing consequences.

Planning and discovery are designed to put you in the right opportunities, those that are well-qualified and create a strong fit for your product or service. Proper attention to these first two phases in the process are critical to creating consistent, long-term success, and also ensure the greatest return on your most important resource—your time.

Effective planning and discovery will not only help you get more hits, but these critical phases of the 1-on-1 Selling™ process will help you hit more doubles and triples and home runs. You will close more deals, and you will increase the size of the deals you close.

This is a critical point for all high-performance salespeople. To reach your income earning potential, your primary objective is not to make as many presentations as possible, but to qualify as many high-value, high-probability opportunities as you can.

In sports, coaches and managers constantly evaluate the game performance of their players. These evaluations are designed to identify the weaknesses in the players' game, to break down the performance into its individual parts and identify areas that are limiting success or creating failure.

Imagine for a moment what it would be like if coaches simply looked at won-lost records and didn't break down the athlete's performance into its process parts. Athletes with winning records would probably be labeled 'born winners' while losing athletes with losing records would be admonished to play harder or something equally helpful.

Salespeople can avoid this problem by following the sales process that is the foundation of 1-on-1 Selling™. In addition to all its other benefits, this sales process will help you to break down your performance into its individual parts and identify any weaknesses you may have in your sales game.

1-on-1 Principle™
A defined sales process provides the most effective use of your most valuable resource—your time.

1-on-1 Principles™

Chapter 11:

Implementing an effective sales process is the key to creating consistent sales performance, and the only way to truly know what is working and what isn't.

Chapter 12:

A defined sales process provides the most effective use of your most valuable resource—your time.

PART IV
PLANNING

CHAPTER 13

PLAN TO WIN

"Have a bias toward action - let's see something happen now.
You can break that big plan into small steps and
take the first step right away."
— *Indira Gandhi*

"Plans are only good intentions unless they immediately
degenerate into hard work."
— *Peter Drucker*

FOUR HUNDRED AND TEN DAYS. That is how long it took to construct the Empire State Building. One year, one month, and fifteen days—start to finish.

Upon completion, the Empire State Building was the tallest structure in the entire world—and remained so for forty years. It was the first building in the world to exceed one hundred floors. It reached 1,453 feet into the New York sky, requiring 57,000 tons of structural steel, 70 miles of pipe, and 2.5 million feet of electrical wire to build.

Yet, incredibly, it took little more than fourteen months to complete.

Dubbed one of the seven wonders of the modern world by the American Society of Civil Engineers, the Empire State Building was envisioned by John J. Raskob and designed by the architectural firm of Shreve, Lamb & Harmon. In his book *Higher: A Historic Race to the Sky and the Making of a City*, Neal Bascomb describes how this legendary team accomplished such an extraordinary feat:

> Shreve, Lamb & Harmon planned out the entire skyscraper before the first story was raised. They knew the number of beams and columns, their lengths, and the amount of bolts and rivets needed to put them together.

> . . . [They] developed . . . a graphical system of events that
> needed to occur simultaneously . . . in order to avoid losing
> one hour, let alone one day, from the schedule. The system
> predated by decades "critical path" techniques that now re-
> quire more technology than penciled drawings on a large
> board—but Shreve's method was no less efficient. Andrew
> Eken said of the firm's superhuman focus on the Empire
> State, "They knew when we would need the electrical layout
> or the plumbing blueprints, for example, and we didn't even
> have to ask. We'd just send a messenger to their office and
> the right number of the right prints would be packed and
> ready for us.

When the Empire State Building was completed in record time, it wasn't an accident. No, the critical aspect of this stunning success— arguably the most important step in the whole process—was the de- velopment of a comprehensive step-by-step plan that perfectly prepared the crew to complete the "mission."

And so it is with the process of building your sales success. To generate consistent sales performance, easily the most important step in the sales process is the first one, the creation of an effective plan to help you identify as many **high-value, high-probability pro- spects** as possible. This, as we will discover, is the key to helping you manage your time much more efficiently.

To achieve both of these objectives, we will do three specific things in the planning phase of the sales process:

1. Use your best accounts to create a profile for the accounts you should pursue.

2. Use that basic profile to "identify" as many potential high- value prospects as possible.

3. Create a "Blueprint" of each of these prospects.

The planning phase of the sales process is designed to put you in those opportunities that give you the very best chance to win. Over the next few chapters, I will outline the details of how this is done and show you how this phase of the sales process will create more wins than you ever imagined.

> **1-on-1 Principle™**
> The planning stage of the 1-on-1 Selling™ process is the single most important tool in building a consistent sales pipeline.

CHAPTER 14

PARETO—A SALESPERSON'S BEST FRIEND

"You hit home runs not by chance, but by preparation."
— *Roger Maris*

"It's not the will to win that matters—everyone has that.
It's the will to prepare to win that matters."
— *Paul "Bear" Bryant*

IN THE 1940s, management consultant Dr. Joseph M. Juran recognized that for many observable events, 80 percent of results stemmed from only 20 percent of the causes. In his writing, he described this phenomenon as the "vital few and trivial many," and attributed the idea to Vilfredo Pareto, an early 20th century Italian economist who had detected that 80 percent of the wealth in his country was owned by only 20 percent of its people.

The 80/20 rule, or Pareto's Law, suggests that many things in life are unequally distributed, that a large percentage of results are typically created by a small percentage of inputs. Not surprisingly, this concept finds application in the business world, where a common rule of thumb is that roughly 80 percent of sales revenue is usually produced by only 20 percent of customers.

This simple principle has tremendous implications for salespeople. Here's why: although salespeople recognize that larger customers typically require more of their time and attention, they will often work very hard to contact and cultivate most every customer on their account list, regardless of sales revenue. Unfortunately, the prospect of adequately maintaining a large number of accounts can be both overwhelming and incredibly frustrating. As an account list grows to a hundred—or hundreds—of customers, there never seems to be enough time to adequately serve them all.

This is where our friend Pareto comes into the picture.

Let's complete an 80/20 analysis of your current customers.* First, obtain (or create) a sales report that lists all of your customers sorted by sales volume, what is typically referred to as a 'Year-to-Date Sales Report by Customer Rank'. This report should list all the customers that have purchased products or services from you this year (or during the last 12 months), beginning with your largest account and progressing to your smallest account.

Once you have that report, find your total sales volume for the time period of the report, multiply that number by 80 percent, and record it.

Now, we will determine how closely the 80/20 rule applies to your sales revenue.

1. Count the total number of customers on your list. Record that number.

2. Go back to your sales report. Begin with your largest customer and work down the list, adding up the sales for each of your accounts until you reach the revenue total calculated above (80 percent of your sales revenue).

3. When you reach that total, draw a line underneath that customer's name that puts you over the top. Then count the number of accounts that you needed to reach 80 percent of your sales revenue. Record that number.

4. Finally, divide the number from No. 1 (the total number of customers on your report) by the number from No. 3 (the number of accounts needed to get to 80 percent of your total revenue). This is the percentage of your accounts needed to reach 80 percent of your sales revenue. What percentage of your accounts does that number represent? How close is it to 20 percent?

You may be wondering why we would take the time to identify your most significant customers, something that must already be quite obvious to you. What you will find is that knowing your most important customers is one thing, but analyzing those customers can produce some very useful information.

First, for discussion purposes, we will label these accounts—the customers that produce 80 percent of your sales revenue—as your KEY accounts. Bear in mind that a "KEY" account means something specific. To be a KEY account, a customer has to produce the amount of revenue that places them in that category—in other words, they have to be among those top accounts that produce the top 80 percent of your revenue.

What you will find is that, as your total sales revenue grows over time, the minimum value of a KEY account will grow with it. Also, a customer that is a KEY account today may eventually fall out of that category while others that are not currently KEY accounts may become so in the future—it all depends on the revenue produced by the customer.

Quite obviously, your KEY accounts are crucial to your continued success. At the same time, the revenue potential they represent means they are coveted by your competitors as well. Clearly, these customers are worthy of a presidential protection detail! Every competitor in your industry would give just about anything (including their own margins, unfortunately) to have these accounts, so you need to develop a clear strategy for enhancing your relationship with them and protecting them from intruders.

Second, analyzing your KEY accounts will lead you to develop a very clear picture of the type of prospects you should be calling on, and why (more in Chapter 15). Since these are your best accounts, you want to analyze them in great detail to determine why you do well with them, and you want to figure out how you can replicate your success with other similar accounts.

Third, you will find that focusing on 20 percent of your accounts is much easier logistically than trying to manage all of them. For instance, if you have 100 accounts, managing 20 of them very closely is much easier than attempting to spend time with all 100. Understand that I am not at all suggesting you ignore the bottom 80 percent of your customers. What I am saying is that when you fully realize that those customers provide only 20 percent of your revenue, it will change the amount of time you invest in them.

One very important point before we continue: each of your customers deserves your company's very best efforts—both in terms of product or service delivery and the service and support they receive after the sale. However, the reason I want you to divide your accounts into different categories is that you need to determine where you can most effectively spend your time—your single most valuable resource.

> **1-on-1 Principle™**
> The 80/20 rule is the key to identifying those high-value, high-probability customers that are most likely to use your products or services.

*To download a form or spreadsheet for your 80/20 customer analysis, visit www.1on1selling.com and click on "Resources."

CHAPTER 15

The Real Value of KEY Accounts

"There is nothing so useless as doing efficiently that which should not be done at all."

— Peter Drucker

"Show me the money!"

— Jerry Maguire

AS A SALESPERSON, given a choice, which would you prefer: to manage 100 customer accounts that produce $1 million in revenue, or only 25 accounts that produce exactly the same amount?

Silly question, right? Twenty-five accounts instead of one hundred for the same revenue? Easy choice.

So, why do most salespeople—in real life—choose the first option? Let me explain.

Revisiting the 80/20 rule, let's assume you have 100 customers that are producing $1 million in total sales revenue. If the 80/20 rule holds true, then $800,000 of your revenue is being created by only 20 accounts—an average of $40,000 per account. Of course, in reality, each KEY account is not generating exactly $40,000—some are producing much more than the average, and others much less—but the average gives you a baseline for comparison.

For example, you will immediately see that the revenue produced by your average KEY account ($40,000) is four times as much as the average of all 100 accounts ($10,000). However, if we go a bit further, you will discover that KEY accounts are even more valuable than you first believe.

Let's calculate the value of the remaining 80 accounts in our illustration. Since these customers do not generate enough revenue to be labeled as KEY accounts, we will differentiate them by labeling them as 'Secondary' accounts. Notice that these Secondary accounts are responsible for only 20 percent of your annual sales revenue—$200,000. This means that each Secondary account produces on average only $2500. Comparing that to your average KEY account ($40,000), we discover an even greater value for your KEY accounts than we first calculated—16 times more revenue on average than your bottom 80 accounts!

With this in mind, where do you think you should you be spending a good deal of your time?

Let's do one more thing to demonstrate how valuable your KEY accounts are. Just for the sake of illustration, consider what the impact would be if, in the exercise above, you lost (or voluntarily gave up) all 80 of those Secondary accounts. You would lose 20 percent of your total revenue, of course, but exactly how many KEY accounts would you need to acquire in order to recoup your losses if, indeed, you lost every single one of those accounts?

The reality is that it would only require five new KEY accounts to replace the entire $200,000 in lost revenue! Five accounts averaging $40,000 in revenue (the average KEY account) would slash your account list from 100 to only 25 while generating the same amount of revenue.

Imagine the impact on your time management!

Before we proceed, let me be crystal clear—I am not actually suggesting that you abandon the bottom 80 percent of your customers. What I am suggesting is that you consider very carefully how you manage your time. Because your time is not limitless, you cannot possibly spend the same amount with every single customer on your list, nor should you! Instead, you should create a strategy for managing and protecting your KEY accounts and a much different strategy for managing and/or developing your Secondary accounts.

THE IMPLICATIONS OF THE 80/20 RULE

After 25 years of training and managing salespeople, I have seen the 80/20 principle consistently apply. It's not always exactly 80/20, of course; sometimes it takes 25 or 30 percent of your customers to reach 80 percent of your revenue, but sometimes it takes as little as 15 percent. Regardless of the exact percentages, this ratio is extremely telling.

If it takes much more than 20 percent of your customers to reach 80 percent of your total revenue, it is very likely that you don't have enough large accounts and you are required to work very hard to produce less revenue than you should. If, however, it takes much fewer than 20 percent of your accounts to produce 80 percent of your revenue, it may mean you have all of your eggs in too few baskets, and your revenue might be at risk.

The vast majority of salespeople, until they understand the implications of the unequal distribution in revenue between KEY accounts and Secondary accounts, try to spend equal amounts of time with all of their customers. With very few exceptions, this is a very bad idea. Now, armed with an understanding of the value of each segment of your customers, you should have three distinct priorities:

1. Protect, maintain, and further develop your KEY accounts.

2. Send the balance of your time doing everything possible to create more of those KEY accounts.

3. Develop a strategy for your Secondary accounts.

In the next chapter we will combine the second and third priorities and discover that the primary strategy for dealing with Secondary accounts is to mine them for potential KEY accounts.

> **1-on-1 Principle™**
> Creating, developing, and protecting KEY accounts is critical to effective time and territory management.

CHAPTER 16

TARGETS OF OPPORTUNITY

"Whenever you want to achieve something, keep your eyes open,
concentrate and make sure you know exactly what it is you want.
No one can hit their target with their eyes closed."
— Paulo Coelho

"Bad decisions made with good intentions are still bad decisions."
— Jim Collins

IN HIS RUNAWAY BEST SELLER, *Good to Great*, author Jim Collins identified eleven companies that, according to his financial criteria, achieved a level of performance over an extended period of time that transcends the marketplace—that made them "great" companies.

Unfortunately, for some of those companies, the road to greatness ended in an off-ramp to disaster. Circuit City went bankrupt. Wells Fargo needed a $25 billion government bailout. Fannie Mae turned into a train wreck as its stock plunged from over $60 to less than $1 and was delisted from the New York Stock Exchange. It seems nothing lasts forever—even for some great companies.

Despite these eventualities, Collins' research lends some critical insights into the differences between an average company and an extraordinary one: Hire the right people. Ensure they are in the right places. Develop humble leaders. Create the right culture. And, perhaps most importantly, understand the "Hedgehog Concept":

> A Hedgehog Concept is not a goal to be the best, a strategy to be the best, an intention to be the best, a plan to be the best. It is an understanding of what you can be the best at. The distinction is absolutely crucial.

The Hedgehog Concept is a direct way of finding out exactly how your company can be most successful and, according the Collins, stems from three simple questions:

1. What can you be best in the world at?

2. What drives your economic engine?

3. What are you deeply passionate about?

The beauty of the Hedgehog Concept is that we can apply a variation of it to your sales approach. Now that you have identified your KEY customers using the 80/20 rule, we can ask three very specific questions to create a clear map of exactly which customers you should be vigorously pursuing and why:

1. What do your best customers want/buy from your company?

2. What do your best customers "look" like?

3. Where can I find more just like them?

Our purpose is quite simple: to take your current success stories (your KEY accounts) and to identify those prospective customers that have the potential to become success stories of their own (new KEY accounts).

THE CORE OF SUCCESSFUL TERRITORY MANAGEMENT

In the last chapter, we established these critical priorities for developing your sales territory after you have identified your KEY accounts:

1. Protect, maintain, and further develop your KEY accounts (top 80 percent of your revenue).

2. Spend the balance of your time doing everything possible to create more of those KEY accounts.

3. Develop a strategy for your Secondary accounts (bottom 20 percent of your revenue).

These three principles are the core of successful territory management. You should prioritize the majority of your time to protect and develop your most important customers and find more just like them. Going forward, the label that we will use for those high-priority prospects we are looking for—those that could become KEY accounts—will be "TARGET" accounts.

Please note that, just like the label "KEY," we use the label "TARGET" to mean something very specific. A TARGET account is not just any prospect that you are working with. It is defined as any prospect that you believe has the potential to generate enough sales revenue to become a KEY account—to move into the top 20 percent of your customers.

Also, remember that the revenue threshold to become a KEY account is not defined by the average revenue of your KEY accounts. It is determined by the revenue of the smallest KEY account. So, using the illustration from Chapter 14, the average revenue of your KEY accounts may be $40,000, but the smallest of your KEY accounts (the last account that puts you over 80 percent of your total revenue) may be quite less ($15,000, for example).

So, your TARGET accounts are those prospects that can potentially produce the minimum threshold of revenue to become a KEY account, and these accounts are your highest priority. Having used the 80/20 principle to identify your KEY accounts, the next step is to use any information or data you can gather from those KEY accounts to understand what your ideal TARGET account should look like. Our objective is to answer our three critical "Hedgehog" questions:

1. What do your best customers want/buy from your company?

2. What do your best customers "look" like?

3. Where can I find more just like them?

The answers to these three questions will lead you to a laundry list of accounts that will ultimately become your TARGET accounts.

To get started in this process, simply analyze your current KEY accounts with the following questions in mind:

- What characteristics are common to a number of my KEY accounts?

- Is there one product or service that seems to do very well in a number of my KEY accounts?

- Is there any specific approach or idea that I have used successfully in acquiring my KEY accounts?

- Is there one competitor's product/service that I have had success in converting to my product/service?

- Is there a buyer with a certain type of background or personal association that prefers my product/service?

If you don't work in a specific industry (the medical market, for example), and your products or services are used in a variety of markets, answer these questions as well:

- Is there a particular industry or market sector that is common to my KEY accounts?

- Is there one type of business that is more common in your KEY accounts?

Asking these questions will help you find any consistencies in your current customers that will point you in a very specific direction to new customers. It is not that you want to exclude any qualified opportunity, but you want to try to identify any existing patterns that will provide you with the very best opportunity to grow your business.

For example, you may find that you have several customers in the medical field or in manufacturing. You may do very well with family-owned businesses or locally-owned companies. Several of your best customers may currently utilize two specific products or services.

You may find that a particular network or referral source has provided many of your best clients. There may, in fact, be several patterns that emerge from your KEY account analysis, and each of these patterns may potentially define a pool of potential high-value, high-probability prospects.

EASY TARGETS

The logical place to look for TARGET accounts is right under your nose! Analyze the large number of accounts that currently produce the bottom 20 percent of your business. You already do business with these customers, and you probably know a great deal about them—the types of products they use, the competitors they buy from, the decision makers, and so on. As you analyze your list of accounts, answer the following questions:

- Do you have any new customers among your Secondary accounts that have only recently been added and have the potential to become a KEY account?

- Do you have any Secondary accounts that could easily purchase additional products or services—or the same products/ services in other departments—but you have failed to create a plan to further penetrate the account? Could they become a KEY account?

- Do you have Secondary accounts with subsidiaries, other business units, other locations, or related businesses that could generate enough business to potentially become a KEY account?

An affirmative answer to any of these three questions automatically elevates that particular Secondary account to a TARGET account! Why? Because that current customer could potentially produce KEY account revenue.

Once you have developed a lengthy list of TARGET accounts, it is time to get busy. The next steps in the planning phase of the sales process is to "blueprint" these accounts, and to qualify them to determine if and how they should be pursued.

> **1-on-1 Principle™**
> Identifying and managing TARGET accounts—prospects that have the potential to become KEY accounts—is the most efficient way to grow and manage your sales territory.

CHAPTER 17

THE DEVIL IS IN THE DETAILS

"Sometimes the situation is only a problem because it is looked at in a certain way. Looked at in another way, the right course of action may be so obvious that the problem no longer exists."
— *Edward de Bono*

"It's the little details that are vital. Little things make big things happen."
— *John Wooden*

YOU HAVE BEGUN TO DEVELOP a plan to grow your business. You have learned to focus on your KEY accounts and your TARGET accounts. At this point, one of the more common errors that salespeople tend to make is to rush headlong into a presentation with a potential customer. The mistake is in thinking that selling is no more complicated than telling your prospect everything there is to know about your company and the products or services you offer.

Unfortunately, the truth is your prospects really don't care about you or your company—at least not at first. What they do passionately care about is purchasing a product or service that will solve their specific problem, although with a few not-so-insignificant conditions:

- They want to buy from a salesperson they like.

- They want to buy from a salesperson they trust.

- They want the transaction to be as painless as possible.

- They want as little change as possible to their organization or internal systems.

- They want to be able to justify the purchase to anyone who might question their decision.

- And, of course, as they will readily tell you, they want the best price.

The point is that before you launch into a boilerplate presentation about your superior products and the great company you work for, consider that your prospects might be much more impressed if you do a little homework to find out about them. As it turns out, a relationship is a lot easier to develop when customers think you have an interest in them and the purpose of your call is not simply an attempt to pad your commission check this month.

Don Rainey is a partner in a prominent venture-capitalist firm specializing in high-potential technology companies. As someone who has seen a sizable number of sales presentations, he offers this advice to entrepreneurs approaching his firm looking for funding:

> One doesn't need be an expert on our history, track record or portfolio but a little knowledge can go a long way. Just a little awareness of our companies, professional background, and current boards can drive efficiency for the person pitching an idea. If I've had three companies in Internet Advertising, for example, you can probably skip explaining simple concepts related to it. If one lacks that awareness, it wastes time AND undermines credibility. Plus, you look like someone who doesn't do what it takes to succeed because, in this instance, you haven't [done what it takes] . . . .

This is fairly straightforward: If you don't do your homework, you undermine your credibility! If you approach your prospects unprepared, they are likely to be irritated, if not outright offended. Further, they may conclude that your lack of preparation is an indication of how you might handle any future problems they would encounter with your product or service.

Clearly, a salesperson that doesn't have a basic understanding of an account is begging to be embarrassed or simply dismissed. This mistake is usually created by ignorance (a lack of training) or laziness (a lack of discipline), but it can be avoided entirely by doing your homework—what I refer to as "blueprinting" the account.

Blueprinting is what you do to acquire as much data as possible about the prospect—the company, the decision makers, the issues they currently face, and much more. The idea is to gain as much insight into the prospect's business as you possibly can before you make the first sales call.

Let's take a look at the information you should attempt to acquire for any significant sales opportunity (your TARGET accounts):

- All relevant account contact information (address, phone, email, etc.)

- Corporate structure—especially as it relates to the decision-makers

- Website URL and all social media connections

- Products/services currently used, and relevant vendors

- Corporate mission, vision, and values

- Cultural norms, business philosophy

- Current organizational goals and/or objectives

- Core marketing strategies

- Primary competitors

Wow! This sure seems like a lot of information to acquire before you even make your first call. However, I hope you see why it is important to spend some time doing your homework before you call on an account that might eventually land in your KEY account list. The bottom line is, if an account is important enough to be a TARGET account, that account is important enough to warrant doing your homework!*

One note to remember: you may not be able to get all this information prior to your first call; in fact, in some instances you may find yourself face-to-face with a world-class prospect before you get the chance to do any blueprinting at all. You might, for instance, get introduced to a key contact at a business function, an industry association meeting, or a trade show. In these circumstances, your first order of business is to ask questions designed to give you insight into the prospect's business rather than launching right into an introduction of your company and its products and services.

CRITICAL BLUEPRINTING INFORMATION

Of all the information to acquire, the most important is the corporate structure of the company—not only to discover who may be involved in the decision-making process, but also to determine if you can identify links into the account. Once you know who works within the TARGET account, your objective is to find someone who might give you a referral, or connect you directly to the decision maker, or provide you with valuable insight into the company.

A cold call can warm up in a hurry if you are able to create these critical connections into the company, and the ability to do this effectively has increased many times over with the introduction of social networking tools, such as LinkedIn, Facebook, and Twitter.

Indeed, technology has opened the floodgates of information available to you. Corporate websites are loaded with useful information—company profiles, vision and mission statements, news and events, press releases, industry links, awards and recognition, newsletters, high-profile customers, contact information, and much more. Plus, you can use your favorite search engine (Google, Yahoo, Bing, etc.) to gather additional information on the account—industry or trade magazine articles, newspaper articles, financial information, and more.

Local newspaper articles are frequently an excellent source of information about individuals in the company who are involved in charity work, community or civic organizations, and other volunteer work. This opens up a whole new vista of opportunity—each of those organizations represents potential network contacts that may create a valuable link into the account.

In review, the purpose of blueprinting is twofold:

1. To identify a potential link into the account—a referral, a personal introduction, or a mutual connection you can reference.

2. To help you better understand the prospect's business so that your presentation can be tailored to the company's needs, culture, and methods of doing business.

Although you have gathered a tremendous amount of information about your prospect, there is still substantial work to be done before you jump into a product presentation. You need to further qualify the opportunity to ensure that you are investing your time wisely, and you need to clearly define the gap your product or service can fill. We will do that, and more, in the next phase of the 1-on-1 Selling™ process.

> **1-on-1 Principle™**
> Doing your homework adds to your credibility, and will likely uncover valuable information you can use later.

*To download a form or spreadsheet that can be used to blueprint your TARGET accounts, visit www.1on1selling.com and click on "Resources."

Also, for more invaluable information about blueprinting, read *Beyond Selling Value: A Proven Process to Avoid the Vendor Trap*, by Mark Shonka and Dan Kosch. Kaplan Business (2002).

1-on-1 Principles™

Chapter 13:
Planning isn't sexy, but it is the single most important tool in building a consistent sales pipeline.

Chapter 14:
The 80/20 rule is the key to identifying those high-value, high-probability customers that are most likely to use your products or services.

Chapter 15:
Creating, developing, and protecting KEY accounts is critical to effective time and territory management.

Chapter 16:
Identifying and managing TARGET accounts—prospects that have the potential to become KEY accounts—is the most efficient way to grow and manage your sales territory.

Chapter 17:
Doing your homework adds to your credibility, and will likely uncover valuable information you can use later.

PART V

DISCOVERY

CHAPTER 18

THE ART OF THE INTERVIEW

> "If you do not ask the right questions, you do not get the right answers. A question asked in the right way often points to its own answer. Asking questions is the A-B-C of diagnosis."
> — *Edward Hodnett*

> "This is a sales pitch. It's not going to be won by the law, it's going to be won by the lawyers."
> — *Lieutenant Kaffee, A Few Good Men*

IF YOU LOVE MOVIES, chances are pretty good that *A Few Good Men* is somewhere in your list of favorites. Jack Nicholson. Tom Cruise. Demi Moore. A great courtroom thriller. What's not to like?

Perhaps you remember this classic exchange between Cruise (Lieutenant Kaffee) and Nicholson (Colonel Jessup):

Jessup:
You want answers?

Kaffee:
I want the truth!

Jessup:
You can't handle the truth!

Son, we live in a world that has walls, and those walls have to be guarded by men with guns. Who's gonna do it? You? You, Lieutenant Weinberg?

I have a greater responsibility than you could possibly fathom. You weep for Santiago, and you curse the Marines. You have that luxury. You have the luxury of not knowing what I know. That Santiago's death, while tragic, probably saved lives. And my existence, while grotesque and incomprehensible to you, saves lives. You don't want the truth because deep down in places you don't talk about at parties, you want me on that wall, you need me on that wall.

We use words like honor, code, loyalty. We use these words as the backbone of a life spent defending something. You use them as a punch line.

I have neither the time nor the inclination to explain myself to a man who rises and sleeps under the blanket of the very freedom that I provide, and then questions the manner in which I provide it. I would rather you just said thank you, and went on your way. Otherwise, I suggest you pick up a weapon, and stand a post.

Either way, I don't give a damn what you think you are entitled to!

Kaffee:
Did you order the Code Red?

Jessup:
I did my job.

Kaffee:
DID YOU ORDER THE CODE RED?

Jessup:
You damn right I did!!

Picture a packed movie theater, and not a single sound from the crowd. You can hear a pin drop. That scene never fails to impress.

But what is the relevance to selling?

Sure, it's fiction, but it mirrors the real world. Hours of preparation went into that decisive moment in the trial. Kaffee understood that he needed critical information from Jessup to make his case, so he prepared extensively to reach a point where he could extract the admission he needed.

The point is, there are some very strong connections between the professions of selling and the law. In American law, discovery is the pretrial phase of a court case that gives involved parties an opportunity to gather relevant information from the opposition. Typically, attorneys are entitled to any materials related to the case, and they may, if necessary, compel the opposing party to provide those materials. In many cases, attorneys conduct personal interviews (depositions) to obtain critical information from an individual who has some bearing on the proceedings.

The discovery phase of the 1-on-1 Selling™ process is very similar, except for one very important point—your prospect cannot be compelled by law to provide you with the information you want! Instead, you have to earn the right to that information.

By that I mean you have to create enough credibility and trust with your prospects so they are comfortable sharing the information you need to move the sale forward. Then, assuming your prospect is willing to share the information you need, you still have to know what information is critical and how to structure your questions to learn what you need to know.

What great salespeople learn is that interviewing skills are just as important as presentation skills! What this means is that salespeople need to master both the ability to ask effective questions and the ability to be a good listener. To that end, a sales manager once told me that a prospect will tell you exactly what you need to know to win a sale if you have enough sense to ask the right questions and are willing to carefully listen to the answers.

The problem is that salespeople often insist on dominating a sales call, talking for as much as 80 percent of their time with the prospect.

In most cases, this happens because they believe that selling is defined as telling the prospect everything they know about their prod-product. For others, it's just a case of nerves; they just can't seem to be quiet for very long. In some cases, in the absence of training, the salesperson simply doesn't know any better. Whatever the cause, salespeople tend to be more comfortable in a sales call when they feel in control, and they are convinced that talking gives them that control.

Unfortunately, they are mistaken. The truth is that control is not gained by telling, but by asking. Effective salespeople, like effective attorneys, recognize that there is enormous power and control in asking the right questions and pursuing the clues given in the answers. However, unlike some manipulative sales techniques (or courtroom tactics) that seek to walk a prospect into a trap, the objective of your questions is not to find a way to use the prospect's words against them. Rather, your objective is to obtain vital information that will help you understand the prospect's motivations for making a purchasing decision, the factors that will impact the final decision, and the barriers you must overcome to get the business.

THE CUSTOMER INTERVIEW

The discovery phase of the 1-on-1 Selling™ process outlines the first few calls on your prospective customer, and these initial calls, or a single call in some cases, are best described as "interview" calls.

The interview call is exactly what it sounds like—your chance to interview the prospect and discover the necessary information you need to make decisions about the opportunity, to continue in the opportunity, or to possibly set it aside in lieu of other opportunities.

Whether it is a cold call, a warm call, or an open-arms invitation from the account, this call (or calls) is designed to 1) provide you with the critical information you need to move the sale forward, 2) define you and your company to the prospect, and 3) set the stage for a powerhouse solution presentation in the future, assuming you choose to move ahead.

Whether it takes one call or more, you will have three distinct objectives during the discovery phase of the 1-on-1 Selling™ process:

1. To "qualify" the prospect.

2. To reveal the prospect's needs.

3. To determine the prospect's agendas for the purchase.

Keep in mind that, as you plan your first few calls, these should be your objectives for the call. When you have completed the discovery phase of the sales process and decide to move forward, it will be because you have determined that the account is qualified, you have identified a credible need, and you understand why the client wants to make a purchase.

We will spend the next several chapters unraveling the details.

> **1-on-1 Principle™**
> In selling, interviewing skills are just as important as presentation skills.

CHAPTER 19

IS YOUR CUSTOMER QUALIFIED?

"Judge a man by his questions rather than his answers."
— *Voltaire*

"An investment in knowledge pays the best interest."
— *Benjamin Franklin*

IT IS A CONSISTENT ACT of human nature for one to take personal credit for success but to blame circumstances or others for any failure. Salespeople are absolutely guilty: When we win a sale, it's because we're good at what we do. When we lose a sale, it's because of the economy—or any one of several other convenient things we can blame.

Because it certainly couldn't be because we did something wrong. Or could it? Examine this list of sales disasters and decide what they all have in common:

- An unknown decision-maker pops up near the end of the sales process and kills the deal.

- You think you have a sale, but find out at the last minute the budget hasn't been approved.

- After your sales presentation, the customer asks why you didn't address a critical issue—an issue you didn't even know about.

- You find the perfect prospect and spend weeks getting the end-user excited about using it, only to find out that the company has a three-year contract with the current vendor.

- After presenting your solution to the prospect, you learn that two competitors are introducing new products for the client to consider.

What do you think? Are these blowouts a failure to present the prospect with the lowest price? Is it poor marketing? Is it the economy? Of course not. In each case, the real culprit is laziness! It is a failure to extract critical account information that eventually derailed the sale.

Unidentified decision makers. Unavailable funds. Unknown issues. New competitors. In each case—and in many other similar failures—the salesperson didn't do his homework. He failed to thoroughly qualify the customer and not only lost the sale, but wasted an enormous amount of valuable time in doing so.

During the first two phases of the sales process (Planning and Discovery), your guiding mission is to qualify the opportunity—to answer a number of key questions regarding the opportunity to determine if it is a good investment of your time, and to determine if the opportunity represents a **high-value, high-probability** account.

Using your time wisely is critically important to your sales success, and qualifying each opportunity is the foundation of managing your time well. Effectively qualifying each prospect will prevent you from wasting valuable time with an account that is unlikely to move forward, and more importantly, keep any last-second surprises from cropping up and jeopardizing the sale.

The five initial qualification criteria you should reference are listed below. Understanding the answers to each of these qualifiers is a must for every TARGET account if you are to fully appreciate and prioritize the opportunity.

- **Potential Needs**
  Do you thoroughly understand the customer's need? Have you identified a performance gap in the current product or service for which you can provide a solution?

- **Current Competitors**
  Do you know the current vendor and/or those vendors that will be competing for the sale? Do you understand what they will offer the customer? Do you have a thorough understanding of the competitors and their competitive advantages?

- **Decision Makers and Other Influencers**
  Do you know all the decision makers and any other individuals who will influence the final decision? These may include any or all of the following: the end-user, the department manager, the financial authority, the information technology manager (if the solution must be integrated into the IT system or has some impact on software, hardware, reporting, etc.), the "final" authority (owner, CEO, president, general manager, etc.), or any other individual or department that might be impacted by your solution.

  This is an area that salespeople tend to neglect. In many cases, there are powerful influencers in a sale that are not readily apparent. They are powerful because the decision maker values their input and places confidence in their opinions. You must diligently search for anyone and everyone that might provide leverage in a sale.

- **Budget**
  Is there a specific amount budgeted for the purchase? Are funds available if a decision is made? Is the prospect dictating terms, pricing, penalties, etc.?

- **Timing of Decision**
  Is the prospect prepared to move forward? Are they just looking, or are they ready to buy? Do they want to implement in stages? Is the decision contingent on some other event? Is there a deadline that is driving the purchase decision? A contract renewal date? A new facility? A project start-up? Is it an end-of-year purchase?

These five criteria are the key indicators for moving forward with a prospect. If any one of these criteria is unknown, it should serve as an immediate red flag—proceed with caution until you have obtained the information. Time after time, salespeople shortcut the qualification criteria and then lose the sale at the end because they missed something important.

Filling in the blanks of these criteria will help you avoid the critical mistakes that can derail a potential sale. In my view, collecting this information should be automatic for every single TARGET account you pursue.

In most cases you will have already begun to acquire this information during the planning phase of the sales process. For example, it is often quite easy to determine the products or services the prospect is currently using, as well as the vendors that supply them (current competitors). More often than not, you will also find out very early who one or more of the decision makers are (decision makers and influencers), although you should never assume that you know all the decision makers until you have thoroughly investigated the account. Another qualification criterion that may surface early on is a contract renewal date or a new budget year (timing of decision).

THE DEATH TRAP

Remember the opening scene in *Raiders of the Lost Ark*? Indiana Jones is deep in the jungle looking for legendary treasure from some long-forgotten culture. As he ventures deep into a cave, he has to negotiate his way past a number of invisible death traps to reach the golden idol.

Qualifying your accounts is like that. One misstep and you're impaled on a spike or full of poisonous darts. Metaphorically, of course.

DANGER! Your biggest challenge may be to have the discipline to qualify every opportunity. It is extremely easy to be unduly influenced by the allure of a "big account" that seems to be on the fast track and skip right over the qualification process. You choose to short-cut the qualification process because you think you have to move quickly or you think things are under control. Then, one foot short of the goal line, the entire deal unravels.

Consistently qualifying your prospects will help you avoid simple mistakes that can kill a golden opportunity. The first time you decide to skip a step, make an assumption, or fail to fill in all the blanks is the one time that giant boulder will roll right over the top of you. Trust me, a little diligence in qualifying will save you a lot of pain.

If you're thinking that sounds like personal experience, you would be correct.

> **1-on-1 Principle™**
> A salesperson's first objective is to identify and thoroughly qualify high-value, high-probability opportunities.

CHAPTER 20

MANAGING YOUR FIRST IMPRESSION

"You persuade a man only insofar as you can talk his language by speech, gesture, tonality, order, image, attitude, idea, identifying your ways with his."
— **Kenneth Burke**

"We simply assume that the way we see things is the way they really are or the way they should be and our attitudes and behaviors grow out of these assumptions."
— **Stephen Covey**

MANY YEARS AGO, while I was working in the orthopedic industry, I had the occasion to meet one of the doctors from an orthopedic clinic in Pine Bluff, Arkansas. I met this particular doctor at an industry convention and he became quite interested in our product line. He ultimately agreed to prescribe one of our products for his next few patients, so I had the company ship the necessary supplies to his office.

A short time later I flew into Little Rock, rented a car, and drove the 45 miles to Pine Bluff in order to work with the first two patients. I was really stoked about the opportunity—and it probably couldn't have gone any worse. Upon arriving, I learned the company had failed to ship the necessary materials required to apply the product, which left me in a very bad situation. I have a physician anxious to try out the product, two patients on hand and in need of the product to continue their rehabilitation, and me with no room to maneuver.

I immediately called the company to explain the dilemma and ask if we had any options whatsoever. I knew the only possible remedy was to get supplies from another customer in the area, but when you're desperate, you start hoping for dramatic rescues. Or miracles.

Or magic dust. Or something. When things are looking bad in front of a customer, you start hoping for that one-in-a-million shot.

Fat chance. Customer Service served up the bad news: find another customer or you're out of luck. Unfortunately, the patients were already in the office waiting, and the nearest customer was almost an hour away in Little Rock—two hours round trip. I was getting nowhere fast and the customer was understandably annoyed.

Frustrated with the failure, I said something on the phone to my Customer Service representative like, "I'm out in the middle of nowhere. I can't just run down the street for supplies." Maybe it was my tone. Maybe it was the words I used. Who knows? But when the nurse manager heard me say, "I'm out in the middle of nowhere,"—completely out of context—she decided I was insulting the doctor and the clinic. She believed that I was characterizing them as small-time, small-town hillbillies, and she was thoroughly offended.

And that was the end of my business in that clinic. I ordered the supplies and, with profuse apologies, reset the appointments. But, when the supplies arrived, they promptly shipped them back and refused to take my calls. It was over a year before I was able to figure out what happened.

In case you're not completely sure yet, first impressions are reasonably important.

GETTING OFF TO A GOOD START

So, you've done a fair amount of homework, and you have a sense of the things you know about the prospect and the things you don't. It's now time to make that all-important first call. This is where you have to pay very close attention, because there are a number of ways to kill a sale before you even get the ball rolling. Trust me, I know.

Dale Carnegie once said, "There are four ways, and only four ways, in which we have contact with the world. We are evaluated and classified by these four contacts: what we do, how we look, what we say, and how we say it." He was alluding to the ways in which we can potentially persuade, or influence in some way, those that we come into contact with.

Conversely, these are the same four ways in which a salesperson can potentially leave a negative impression without intending to do so:

- What we do
- How we look
- What we say
- How we say it

For instance, some salespeople make the mistake of becoming too familiar with a prospect right away, acting as if they are old friends who routinely tell each other everything—shortly after shaking hands for the very first time. This would be an example of **what we do** that might leave a negative impression.

Occasionally, salespeople are guilty of believing their freedom of expression shouldn't influence a buyer's opinion. So, we disregard what people may think and decide that 12 earrings or sleeve tattoos or purple hair shouldn't matter to a customer. Unfortunately, the reality is that people do consistently judge a book by its cover. This would be an example of **how we look** that might leave a negative impression.

Some salespeople fall prey to the bad habits of openly criticizing a competitor or spreading industry rumors or using language the prospect feels is inappropriate. This could be an example of **what we say** or **how we say it** that might leave a negative impression.

The point is that your first impression, if done poorly, can serve as a quick ticket to your dismissal as a serious candidate to do business with the prospect. This is not moralizing; this is Human Relations 101. If you want to persuade people to enter into a business relationship with you, you are going to have to consider their values and norms and be willing to respect them. Not adopt them, or even agree with them, but simply be respectful of them.

Remember, people buy from people they like and trust!

Since our objective is to create a positive first impression with our prospects, it is important to double-check a few critical items before we make our sales call:

- Is your appearance professional and appropriate for the prospect's business environment?

- Are you equipped with the appropriate business tools—business cards, notebook, iPad, brochures, and other collateral materials?

- Do you know how to say your contact's name correctly? Most of the time, prospects will offer their names in the introduction. If not, simply say, "I suspect your (first or last) name could be pronounced a couple of different ways, and I'd like to get it right the first time. Can you help me out?"

- Respect has never gone out of style, and courtesy is always appropriate. Ask for permission rather than make assumptions. Say thank you. Learn how to shake hands properly. Put your cell phone into silent mode.

- Smile and present yourself positively. Avoid whining or complaining about the weather, the economy, or anything else. Chances are you might be the only positive person they see that day, and too many salespeople start off a sales call complaining about something!

Make no mistake, selling is tough enough without sabotaging your own efforts. Make sure you give yourself a chance to connect with your prospect by creating a positive and productive first impression.

1-on-1 Principle™
You only get one chance to make a first impression. It can make or break a sale.

CHAPTER 21

THE INITIAL SALES CALL

"Purpose doesn't make the decision easier, it makes it clearer."
— Roy Spence

"You can close more business in two months by becoming interested in other people than you can in two years by trying to get people interested in you."
— Dale Carnegie

ONE OF THE REASONS business people dread salespeople is the first few minutes of a sales call. Although there are some people who really do like to chat about their favorite sports team, or the weather, or that family picture on the desk, most prospects would like to get down to business. Like you, their most precious commodity is their time, and they really have no interest in wasting it.

This means that the way you handle the first few minutes of the call is critical in identifying yourself as a business professional.

Certainly, a pleasant greeting and introduction are in order. If the prospect responds with small talk, use good judgment in forming a response. Small talk is the socially acceptable way of breaking the ice in a polite fashion; it is not an invitation to prattle on and on, or to assume that you are suddenly long-lost friends. If you were referred by a mutual acquaintance, take the opportunity to make mention of that individual. "I really appreciate John's introduction (or referral). How long have you known each other (or worked together, or been in the same group, or whatever commonality joins them)?"

Then, once your greetings and small talk are concluded, begin by offering your prospect the reason(s) for your call—your Call Purpose. Here is a simple version:

"Tom, thank you for your time. I wanted to meet with you and introduce myself, and talk about (a concept, an idea, or a specific benefit of your product or service)."

Option 1: "Based on what I know about you, I think there may be an opportunity to (describe a significant benefit your company might provide, or a performance gap you might address)."

Or, use **Option 2**, if you were referred or the prospect contacted you with interest: "My understanding is that you may have an interest in (a concept, an idea, or a specific benefit of your product or service)."

"But, with your permission, I would like to take a few minutes to learn more about your current situation. Would that be okay?"

This simple opening creates a clear context for the call and tells your prospect exactly what you hope to accomplish. It focuses the call on the prospect and his needs—not on you and your company. If your proposed benefit or competitive advantage is compelling, and the prospect has any kind of need, chances are good that he will be interested in hearing what you have to say.

It is important to understand the reason for stating your Call Purpose. This statement of purpose is much like the headline of a good story—it is designed to capture the prospect's interest and create the desire to hear more. The most important component of your "headline" is the significant benefit you might provide or performance gap you might address—the concept, idea, or specific benefit.

Please note the focus on the last phrase in the approach outlined above. Your objective is to take a few minutes to learn more about their current situation. This sounds much warmer and much more personal than saying, "I want to ask you some questions." We will discuss the need to avoid an all-out interrogation in the next chapter, but it is important to create dialogue with your prospect rather than a cross examination.

The idea of learning about the prospect's current situation is also very important because things change! It is not at all uncommon to acquire information that is no longer applicable or relevant. Decision makers change. Business objectives change. Budgets get revised. Buying criteria evolve. It is always a good idea to avoid assumptions and confirm critical information as you proceed.

Here, for example, is how a salesperson from a printing company might open an interview call:

> "John, I appreciate your time today. I wanted to talk to you briefly about large format printing for your engineering drawings. Based on what I know now, I think we may be able to reduce your turnaround time on large format printing by two or three days. But, with your permission, I would like to take a few minutes to learn more about your current situation. Would that be okay?"

It doesn't matter if you are selling to an individual buyer, or if you are involved in a complex transaction with several decision makers and a long buying cycle. Opening your conversation with a statement of your Call Purpose gives everyone an agenda to work from. Here is an example from the insurance industry, which typically involves many more decision makers and a more complex buying cycle:

> "Thanks to all of you for your time this morning. I would like to talk with you about the ways we can bring our "local company" focus to your business while, at the same time, offering you "big company" management tools to give you considerably more control over your premium costs. But, with your permission, I would like to take a few minutes to learn more about your current situation. Would that be okay?"

The key is to do good research during the planning phase and customize your benefit to a need or a gap that will capture the prospect's interest. Whether you are asking for an appointment or kicking off an interview call, this opening sets the prospect at ease. It gets the call moving right away and provides answers to most, if not all, of the following questions:

- Why are you making the call?
- Why should I meet with you?
- What benefits will be discussed?
- What problem(s) are you addressing?

More importantly, you set the expectation that the conversation will be about the prospect—not you. Keep in mind that the average salesperson will typically open a sales call with a 20-minute monologue that describes, in painful detail, the company's capabilities, product lines, industry awards, performance history, and so forth. Within a few minutes, the prospect has checked out of the call, thinking about all the things that need to be done. Instead of thinking about your company, he is checking email and devising a polite strategy to cut the call short (sometimes it isn't all that polite!).

Perhaps you have experienced the result of this blunder. It sounds like this: "Thanks for stopping by. Do you have some information you can leave?" or something similar. Regardless, your time, your most precious commodity, has been completely wasted and you've blown what may have been an excellent opportunity.

At this point, your prospect really doesn't have any reason to care about your company. He or she is probably trying to fit this sales call in around a thousand other things that need attention, so there certainly isn't any spare time available just to talk about you. What your prospect might be willing to talk about is the challenges he has, the issues he is contending with, and the problems he needs to solve.

To open your call, use the Call Purpose outline, and then immediately follow up with a strategic dialogue question (see Chapter 23).

Not only will it get your call off to a great start, you will immediately gain credibility with the prospect.

1-on-1 Principle™
A clear agenda for the discovery call will set your prospect at ease.

CHAPTER 22

SKIP THE INTERROGATION

"A prudent question is one-half of wisdom."
— *Francis Bacon*

"All we want are the facts, ma'am."
— *Joe Friday, Dragnet*

BY NOW YOU SHOULD clearly see that, in the world of selling, information is everything. Depending upon the complexity of your product or service, you might need the answers to, literally, dozens of questions. In complex sales, or in opportunities with multiple competitors, or in accounts with multiple decision makers (or influencers), failing to secure even one piece of critical information could be the difference between a win and a disappointing loss with no visible explanation.

In most sales opportunities, there is a mountain of data to be considered and a number of variables to be weighed, so a salesperson must become very adept at asking good questions! However, it's not just the questions themselves; it is the ability to ask questions and elicit information in a natural, conversational style.

No one likes to be interrogated.

This is a minor point with major implications. It means if your typical sales call sounds like a policeman grilling a criminal suspect, your results are probably going to be disappointing. There is, in fact, considerable skill and patience involved in sustaining a productive dialogue that necessarily includes a lot of questions.

Plowing through a list of questions in rapid-fire sequence can put a serious damper on a normal conversation. If you're not sure you agree, try it at home with your spouse or kids and see how they react. Just ask question after question until they throw something at you.

Here is how it might sound in a sales call:

"Which model do you use?"

"How long have you had it?"

"Who did you buy from?"

"What do you like about it?"

"Did you purchase or lease?"

"Did you purchase the extended warranty?"

"How often does the product have to be serviced?"

"Have you budgeted for a replacement?"

"Is there an existing contract? When does it expire?"

"Will you make this decision, or will others be involved?"

"Are others competitors being considered? Who are they?"

"Who will be involved in making this decision?"

"Who will ultimately use the product?"

"What specific problems are you trying to solve?"

"Are you replacing or upgrading your current product?"

"How will the buying process work?"

"Do you want to lease or purchase?"

"Will you need on-site technical support?"

You get the idea. About half-way through this list of questions the prospect will start to fidget. By the time you have reached the last question, the prospect will be ready to strangle you. Remember this: While the interview call is about gathering information, it is equally about creating a highly favorable credibility picture for you and your company. It would be a shame to lose the momentum you have worked so hard to create by turning the call into a hard-core interrogation.

High-performance salespeople make the discovery call look easy not because they are "born salespeople," but because they invest a lot of time and effort in preparation. If your current style of preparation is to grab a brochure and a product sample on the way out the door and 'wing it' during the sales call, it may explain why your sales calls consistently fail to produce quality results.

Skilled salespeople learn how to weave key questions into an easy dialogue with the prospect. As the call progresses, they pay careful attention to the prospect's body language. Do the answers come easily and naturally? Does the prospect appear comfortable? Does the prospect appear engaged? Has the dialogue reached a natural stopping point?

In any event, an experienced salesperson is clued in to the customer and recognizes when it is time to wrap up a call and decide on the next steps.

1-on-1 Principle™
An interrogation is the last thing any prospect wants to endure.

CHAPTER 23

A SUCCESSFUL SALE STARTS WITH A CONVERSATION

"Ideal conversation must be an exchange of thought, and not, as
many of those who worry most about their shortcomings
believe, an eloquent exhibition of wit or oratory."
— *Emily Post*

"Even though we may feel that we are listening very hard, what we
are usually doing is listening selectively, with a present agenda
in mind, wondering as we listen how we can achieve certain
desired results and get the conversation over with
as quickly as possible, or redirect it in ways
more satisfactory to us."
— *M. Scott Peck*

ONE OF THE PRINCIPAL PRODUCTS I sold in the orthopedic industry was a custom-fabricated knee brace that patients wore to stabilize
their damaged or surgically-repaired knees. I had, in fact, been one of
those patients. Prior to joining the company, I had torn the ACL (an-
terior cruciate ligament) in my right knee, and subsequently injured
my left knee a few years later. Both injuries required ACL reconstruc-
tive surgery, and I needed to wear a knee brace during sporting
activities for quite some time.

As you observe athletes wearing knee braces during competition,
one of the things you quickly notice is that brace movement on the
leg is a consistent and significant problem. During rigorous activity,
as gravity and leg motion work together, a knee brace will typically
start to migrate down the leg. The challenge of keeping a knee brace
properly positioned on the leg is inconvenient at best and incredibly
irritating at worst.

It was this one issue that provided me with an amazing competitive advantage in the orthopedic community. Our product was specifically designed with a patented suspension system that eliminated brace slippage as an issue. The impact on both patient and physician was considerable—comfortable, hassle-free wear for the patient, far fewer complaints from dissatisfied patients for the physician.

The challenge was how best to introduce this advantage to the orthopedic surgeon.

I finally hit upon a powerful question that I used very successfully to create a natural dialogue with doctors. After introducing myself and communicating the purpose for my call, I would simply ask this question: "Doctor, in your experience, what do all ACL knee braces have in common?" This turned out to be an extremely effective question because it didn't ask the doctor to critique his current product, but it still asked for his opinion—something, in my experience, most doctors were more than willing to share.

At the time, there was considerable debate in the orthopedic community about the value and effectiveness of knee braces. Physicians had to balance a number of issues in choosing to prescribe a brace for a patient: protecting the surgically-repaired knee after an expensive surgery, getting the patient back to normal activity (including sports) as soon as possible, and containing the patient's out-of-pocket expenses. One thing was clear—if a patient disliked a brace for any reason and it cost the patient a lot of money, the doctor was the prime target for patient complaints.

So, whether the response was delivered sarcastically or seriously, I typically received one of three answers to my question:

- "They don't work."

- "They cost too much."

- "Patients complain about them all the time."

The value of my opening question was that it always led to a discussion of one (or more) of these core issues, and eventually the conversation would turn to the slippage issue where I could clearly differentiate my product from the competition.

THE STRATEGIC DIALOGUE QUESTION

John "Grizz" Deal has been touted as a 'super-salesman' by Inc. magazine. The aptly named 'Deal' is the CEO of Hyperion Power Generation, a start-up company that sells a very unique product—a small, simple nuclear power plant that looks very much like a large diesel engine. Here is how he describes his approach to a sales call:

> I try to keep things relaxed—let's just talk. But I don't need to know if he's married, and I don't want to seem like I'm trying to be his best friend. You want to get to the point where they feel emotionally committed to a partnership. But that's a process, and you have to let them feel they're controlling it. My role in the beginning of the meeting is to say just enough to get them talking, and once they start talking, I shut up.

Get them talking and "shut up"—best advice ever. What book on sales doesn't discuss listening at length? However, while most salespeople need to listen more, the more difficult question is this: How do you get your prospect talking?

As strange as that question may seem, it comes up a lot. Salespeople often complain that they can't get their prospects to open up and share critical information. In my experience, the challenge is that salespeople are often guilty of asking the wrong kinds of questions, questions that inevitably lead to an interrogation:

> What product do you use now?

> Who is your current vendor?

> How often do you order?

While these questions may need to be answered, your first objective is to get your prospect talking about core issues, and the best way to do that is to turn the call over to the prospect right away. After you state the purpose for your call (see Chapter 21), immediately follow up with a strategic dialogue question. This question is designed specifically to open up the conversation with your prospect and elicit personal opinions.

Here are some examples:

- How do you think your company is different from those companies you compete with? What gives you an edge?

- What is the biggest challenge you've encountered in trying to achieve your objectives this year?

- If you could draw things up exactly the way you want, what would you change in your company?

- How is the current economy impacting your ability to (fill in the blank)?

From a printing company salesperson:

- What is the biggest challenge you face in reproducing engineering drawings?

- If you could improve on the process you use to reproduce drawings in your engineering department, what would you most like to change?

- How do you balance the cost of color printing against the volume of copies required in a typical presentation binder?

From an insurance salesperson:

- Do you feel like you have a sense of the internal factors that impact premium costs?

- How effective has your wellness program been in engaging your employees and controlling costs?

- How do you approach balancing costs against adding benefits for employees?

The objective here is simple: Ask an insightful question, and then shut up and listen! Let the prospect describe the issues he or she is facing, but resist the urge to jump in and start fixing things right away. If you listen carefully, the answers will almost always reveal the opportunities you are looking for, or divulge lines of inquiry that you should pursue.

What I have found is that the hallmark of successful salespeople in every industry is the ability to transform a sales call into a natural conversation. Like any conversation, there is a comfortable give-and-take between the salesperson and the prospect, and the exchange is punctuated with open-ended questions that inevitably reveal deeper issues and create further understanding between the two parties.

The key to a great dialogue is finding the right question.

1-on-1 Principle™
Getting your prospect talking is the key to unlocking the door to a sale.

CHAPTER 24

FILLING IN THE BLANKS

"The most successful people in life are generally those who have the best information."
— *Benjamin Disraeli*

"If there are no stupid questions, then what kind of questions do stupid people ask? Do they get smart just in time to ask questions?"
— *From a Dilbert cartoon, by Scott Adams*

EARLY IN MY SALES CAREER I attended a corporate two-week sales training class for new salespeople in Baltimore, Maryland. It was excellent training, and it had a little bit of everything: product knowledge, role play, selling skills training, a presentation project, and much more.

Participants were thoroughly prepped by their managers to do well at the class because each session produced two highly sought-after awards: Most Valuable Player and Best Final Presentation. Winning one of these awards carried a lot of prestige, not just for the salesperson, but also for the sales manager and the region the salesperson represented.

Prior to the training class, my sales manager warned me that in the first session on the very first day, the trainer would ask each salesperson to do an impromptu role-play sales call. Wouldn't you know, lucky me, I was chosen to go first.

Fortunately, I was prepared.

My manager had coached me on how to breeze through this nerve-wracking "test" with flying colors. What he said was simple: When you are given the role-play scenario, you will get only a couple of minutes to prepare. Read the scenario carefully and determine quickly what you know and what you need to know. Then, write down two or three open-ended questions that will start up a conversation and help you fill in the blanks.

Once you ask a question, he said, quit thinking about what to say next and just listen very, very carefully to the answers you receive. As you begin to understand the scenario, use the information you gather to create a solution that makes sense for the opportunity. Those first questions, he emphasized, are the keys to success, if you ask the right questions and pay close attention.

Using his advice, I not only did well in that first test, but I ultimately used the same advice to win the highly coveted Best Final Presentation award.

The Most Important Skill

Most salespeople, and quite a few sales managers, would suggest that listening is the one critical skill that determines the difference between occasional and consistent success. It is hard not to agree with this principle; after all, the salesperson who can obtain the best information will typically win the most sales.

However, the importance of listening is completely dependent upon a much more critical skill—the ability to ask the right questions. Yes, being a great listener is important, but if you're asking bad questions, or the wrong questions, the information you gain isn't valuable—and in selling, information is everything.

This places enormous importance on your ability to ask the right questions, but few salespeople take the time to prepare for the call by thinking about which questions will be the most effective. Winging it—shooting from the hip—is risky at best, and suicidal at worst. The very best way to create a dialogue that reveals the information you need to win the sale is to have the right questions prepared prior to the call.

Michael McLaughlin is a principal in MindShare Consulting LLC, a firm that provides innovative sales and marketing ideas for professional services companies. He argues that salespeople can design the perfect sales questions every time if they will simply take the time to prepare:

> The quality of the work you do before a sales meeting determines the quality of your questions during the meeting. Great preparation on the fundamentals will free up the mental bandwidth you need to focus on nuances about the client's needs that will elude the less-prepared seller.

In other words, if you prepare well, you will spend much less time in the sales call thinking about the questions you need to ask. Your questions will be focused on the critical issues and you won't stumble over the phrasing. Most importantly, since you're not worried about what to say next, you can concentrate on the answers.

CREATING GOOD QUESTIONS

Creating the right questions is a fairly straightforward process: Take what you currently know about the prospect's business and compare it to what you need to know, with special focus on finding performance gaps (Chapter 26) and discovering the buyer's personal agenda (Chapter 32). Once you know where the gaps in your knowledge exist, begin to create possible lines of inquiry that will allow you to fill in the gaps in your current knowledge. Then, work through your ideas and prioritize them for the sales call.

McLaughlin provides clarification on this process:

> Assume, for example, that you are meeting to discuss ways to help a client reduce spending on corporate travel. Based on your research, you might come up with five to eight possible reasons why expenses for corporate travel are on the rise. Your list won't be complete, or always right, but it's a good start.

Then, for each hypothesis, think about a question or two that will help you confirm its validity or suggest another path of inquiry. Don't expect to test every hypothesis during a single meeting, and don't worry if you have more questions than you can ask. You're likely to discover the heart of the matter before you get to all those questions.

If you find yourself wondering how successful salespeople make it look so easy, you've found your answer. Good preparation for a sales call is as easy as thinking through the possibilities. What are the gaps in my understanding of the prospect's needs? What questions could I ask to create a dialogue? How might the customer respond? What possible follow-up questions might that lead to?

It is more work to be well prepared, but the payoff is worth the effort.

> **1-on-1 Principle™**
> Knowing which questions to ask is critical. Making them up on the spot is not such a good idea.

CHAPTER 25

NO CREDIBILITY, NO SALE

"Baldwin had concluded over a whirlwind few days that she had little choice but to resign—because, as she was told, significant discrepancies in one's self-supplied biography were at odds with a movement that promotes integrity and ethics."

— From a Los Angeles Times story regarding
Sandra Baldwin's resignation
as president of USOC

"It takes 20 years to build a reputation and 5 minutes to ruin it. If you think about that, you'll do things differently."

— Warren Buffett

IN DECEMBER 2001, George O'Leary resigned as the head football coach of the Notre Dame Fighting Irish. He held that prestigious position for exactly five days. As it turns out, lying on your resume is not a very good idea. Perhaps you find that to be obvious, but it doesn't appear that word has gotten around.

The following year, Sandra Baldwin was compelled to resign her post as president of the United States Olympic Committee (USOC). Her resume claimed that she had graduated from the University of Colorado and received a doctorate degree from Arizona State. The fact that neither was true was just a minor detail that, in her opinion, could be overlooked. She pleaded her case in a 2002 interview:

> I do not feel I have hurt the credibility of the USOC. I have certainly hurt my own, and I ask you to carefully consider the best course of action for the organization.

They considered. She left.

And there was Kenneth Lonchar (Veritas). And Ronald Zarrella (Bausch & Lomb). And Laura Callahan (Homeland Security). And Robert Irvine (Food Network). And Scott Thompson (Yahoo). They all misrepresented their accomplishments on their resumes.

Which, as you probably suspect, is generally not good for one's credibility.

For the professional salesperson, credibility is everything. In Chapter 20, I shared a story in which one action—what should have been a completely harmless telephone conversation—completely killed a sales opportunity for me. It was completely unintentional, and not something I could have anticipated, but it demonstrates how managing your credibility, from first impression to long-term relationship, is always a concern for the professional salesperson.

Consider this classic example of how salespeople make stupid credibility mistakes. Have you ever walked onto a car lot and been greeted with these classic words: "What do I need to do to get you into a car today?"

This throw-away question is so common that comedian Jerry Seinfeld used it as a parody in a Seinfeld episode. Seinfeld fans may remember a scene in a car dealership where Jerry is sitting with Elaine and her high-fiving boyfriend, Puddy, and Jerry asks, "Now, what do I have to do to put you two in a relationship today?"

Pretty fun in a sitcom. Completely brainless in selling.

The problem is that this common blunder violates a timeless selling principle: people buy from people they like and trust. Unfortunately, thirty seconds onto the car lot, you already don't like the salesperson. Why? Because he is only interested in getting what he wants, and he doesn't want to waste his time making me comfortable or learning anything about me.

In fact, the answer to the question, "What do I need to do to get you into a car today?" is glaringly obvious: "Give me the car I want, with the options I want, at the price I want."

But didn't the salesperson know that already?

ESTABLISHING YOUR CREDIBILITY

Human nature is pretty simple. When a buyer is intent on making a sizeable purchase, or is planning to buy a product or service repeatedly over the long-term, or will have to rely on a company for after-sale maintenance and support, that buyer will have to be convinced that the vendor can be trusted to provide exactly what they claim to provide. There is too much at stake to simply hope for the best.

That means a salesperson must have solid credibility with a prospect before launching into a sales presentation. In essence, a salesperson has to 'earn the right' to do business with the prospect.

So, what are the critical issues in establishing your credibility as you move forward? How do you make the move from being 'just another salesperson' to a salesperson with whom the prospect is sincerely interested in doing business?

Here are eight key factors that impact your credibility with a prospect:

1. The credibility you receive if you are referred by a trusted colleague or friend of the prospect.

2. Your reputation (or your company's reputation), if known.

3. Your professionalism and approach.

4. The value given to you when you know and understand the prospect's business.

5. The demonstration of your industry knowledge.

6. The demonstration of your knowledge of the product and its various applications.

7. Your experience in the industry and previous successes.

8. Your personal credentials and capabilities.

As a salesperson, you have to be concerned with each one of these factors. The very best scenario is one in which you are referred to the prospect. The next best is to have a strong reputation prior to your first visit. Arriving at your first call as a known quantity means that you begin the call with a good amount of credibility already on deposit.

However, if you were not referred or the prospect is learning about you for the very first time, this initial call is your proving ground. The last thing you want is to lose a sale simply because you failed to sufficiently establish your credibility.

By the way, one of the ways salespeople tend to get ahead of themselves is to jump directly to the sales presentation without having done sufficient discovery. Seeing a potential fit for their product or service, salespeople often launch directly into a presentation without a clear understanding of the issues that will influence the final decision.

Which, to the prospect, sounds a lot like this: "Hey, what do I need to do to get you into a sale today?"

1-on-1 Principle™
Don't get ahead of yourself. No credibility means no sale.

CHAPTER 26

HIDDEN TREASURE

"Every sale has five basic obstacles: no need, no money, no hurry, no desire, no trust."

— *Zig Ziglar*

"Listen for hints to things that limit the buyer's ability to use the competition. Look for clues to the time pressures or problems the buyer may be confronting. Listen for clues to what other people in the buyer's organization may think of your product. Listen for all the things you may have going for you, things that strengthen your negotiation position."

— *Gary Karrass*

THERE ARE SEVERAL BARRIERS standing between you and a sale. According to legendary sales trainer, Zig Ziglar, there are five: a need for your product, the ability to pay, a sense of urgency, a desire for the product, and trust in you, the salesperson. While resolving each of these issues is critical in moving the sales process forward, in my opinion, the first of those obstacles is the most critical.

You can't even get started if the prospect doesn't have a need; in fact, the other four obstacles won't even come into play. A prospect must have a need or, at minimum, very quickly perceive a need, or any potential sale is dead on arrival. Your challenge is to help the customer understand that what they need is your product or service.

In my experience, to make that eventuality more likely, you need to find and exploit a performance gap, which is the difference between what the prospect is currently experiencing and what he or she would experience after choosing your solution.

Jim Koch is the Founder and Chairman of the Boston Beer Company, purveyor of the highly successful Samuel Adams brand of beers. When Koch started the company in 1984, he viewed sales "as a slightly questionable act that involved separating people from their money." Fortunately, it didn't take long for him to realize that the beer wasn't going to sell itself, or, as he accurately points out, you "can't sell beer from a desk."

Now, nearly three decades later, the company has over 800 employees and upwards of $500 million in annual revenue, and Koch readily admits that "without sales, there is no business to manage."

In the early days of the business, going from one bar to the next to sell Samuel Adams Boston Lager, Koch quickly latched on to the value of exploiting a performance gap:

> The essence of selling is figuring out how what you're offering will help customers accomplish their objectives—not your objective, their objectives. Anything else is pointless and self-serving. When I walk into a bar, I have about 30 seconds to understand the economics of the place: What is its strategy, and who are the clientele? How does it make money? What's the weakest draft line, **and how would sales increase if we replace it with one of ours?** (emphasis added)

This is where salespeople often lose traction. They look at a prospect using a product or service like theirs and see nothing more than an opportunity to sell a similar product or service. Successful salespeople, on the other hand, see the same opportunity and immediately begin to search for ways to provide something more—to solve a problem, to provide a greater return on investment, to decrease costs, to provide benefits not currently possible with their current solution.

In fact, the bigger the perceived gap, the better the opportunity to make a sale, assuming the costs do not outweigh the realized benefits for the prospect.

Here are examples of areas where performance gaps can be identified:

- A similar product/service but with greatly improved performance

- New or different product features with new or different benefits

- A solution with new or additional applications

- A solution that addresses a currently unresolved challenge or issue

- A solution that is more efficient or more productive, or lowers operating costs

- A solution that increases sales

- A solution that lowers the total cost of ownership

- More extensive inventory availability

- Quicker delivery or turnaround

- Superior warranty coverage

- Additional support services—design, implementation, maintenance, service, training, etc.

In short, a performance gap is any area you identify that will save a prospect time or money, increase revenue, trim expenses, or solve a problem that negatively impacts the company. If your company provides better product availability or delivery, offers more comprehensive after-sale support, includes better training or after-sale support, or bundles additional services, these things represent significant opportunities to create a performance gap for a prospect.

However, one word of warning: any gap you identify must be something the prospect is truly interested in or it has no value.

Here is a four-step process to creating a list of potential performance gaps for any prospect:

Step 1: Clearly define your prospect's current solution.

Step 2: Outline the new or different benefits the prospect will enjoy with your solution. This includes any new or different product/service features that provide tangible benefits to the prospect, or any aspect of your product that will make money, save money, or solve a specific problem for the prospect.

Step 3: Look at the prospect's current results from their solution, and record the strengths and weaknesses of those results. Use this analysis to create a list of positive changes in those results that your solution will provide. What new results, and corresponding benefits, will your solution offer?

Step 4: Identify the prospect's desired results. This is most easily done by asking: "What is the most critical thing you want to accomplish in making a change?" or "What specific improvements are you looking for in a new product/service?" or "Are there any specific problems you are hoping to solve?"

Remember, a performance gap is only valuable if your prospect perceives that it has value, so the list you create from the process above should result in a number of questions to ask during the discovery process. You need to determine the level of interest the prospect has in these potential performance gaps, and, ultimately, you will build your solution presentation around the benefits that create the most enthusiasm.

A couple of warnings: First, you never want to move into a full-blown product or service presentation until you have a clear idea of the most compelling reasons the prospect has for pursuing your solution. Second, you should always be aware that different decision makers (or influencers) will place varying levels of importance on different aspects of your solution. That means you always have a better chance of winning the sale when you clearly understand exactly what is important, and to whom.

1-on-1 Principle™
Performance gaps are a key to creating enthusiastic interest in your product or service.

CHAPTER 27

You Feel Me?

"When dealing with people remember you are not dealing with
creatures of logic, but creatures of emotion."

— *Dale Carnegie*

"People don't ask for facts in making up their minds. They would
rather have one good, soul-satisfying emotion
than a dozen facts."

— *Robert Keith Leavitt*

FANS ARE OFTEN SHOCKED when superstar collegiate athletes decline the opportunity to turn pro and earn millions of dollars, choosing instead to return to college and compete for another year in the NCAA.

Which, in case you're not up to speed, pays nothing (theoretically, at least).

At the end of the 2011 football season, junior USC quarterback Matt Barkley was projected as a top pro prospect who would inevitably sign a multimillion-dollar contract to play in the National Football League. Barkley had finished the season with over 3,500 yards passing and 39 touchdowns, and led the Trojans to a 10-2 record and a No. 6 ranking in the final AP poll.

Despite his accomplishments and the lure of big money, Barkley decided to return to USC for his senior year. But why?

> "Almost everybody goes for the money and the fame that goes along with being a top-five pick in the draft," [USC Head Football Coach Lane] Kiffin said. "That was not very high on his list. He wanted to finish what he started and do something special."

It might appear to an impartial observer that this choice makes little, if any, sense. Barkley could choose fame, financial security, and the opportunity to play in the NFL, or he could stay in school, risk injury, and forfeit a multimillion-dollar payday.

Such is the power of emotion in any decision-making process. Barkley went to USC for the opportunity to continue in a long tradition of football success at the university—to play in the Rose Bowl, to win a national title, to compete for a Heisman Trophy.*

What value do you put on those things?

SELLING IS NOT DEBATING

When I first started selling, I viewed my objective in very simple terms. Each opportunity was a contest where the best presentation— in my view, the best argument—would win the sale. My job was to 'debate' the competition, to position my product against the competition in the very best light, maximizing its strengths and minimizing any real or perceived weaknesses.

At the same time, I had to subtly shine the light of day on my competitor's solution, highlight its glaring weaknesses and simultaneously dismiss its strengths as insignificant. Clearly, my approach to selling assumed that the buyer would make a decision based solely on a clear, logical presentation of facts.

Unfortunately, my prospects didn't always go along.

After losing out on several opportunities that I felt I should've won, I slowly began to catch on to the idea that there are a number of factors that influence a prospect's buying decision, and many of those factors are not—strictly speaking—all that logical. I wasn't sure what those factors were exactly, but it was clear that pure logic was not the sole determinant in most buying decisions. Even when the prospect insisted that price, for example, was the sole consideration for a purchase, I often found that wasn't exactly true.

Still, all things being equal, I stubbornly held on to the belief that the best product or service solution would inevitably win the day, and sometimes that seemed to be true. Frequently, however, I found myself coming away from an opportunity as second-best, losing to a product or service that I knew wasn't as good technically as the one I was offering.

It was about that time that I began reading Zig Ziglar's classic sales book, *Ziglar on Selling*, and the lights started to come on. It was the first time that I seriously considered that emotion might play a role in a prospect's decision.

On the other hand, if we use only logical questions (which the prospects answer out of their intellect), we might well educate them about their needs and the benefits of our product or service, but there is a strong likelihood that they will go down the street and buy from someone who gets them emotionally involved in the benefits of the product. Therefore, it behooves us to combine both emotion and logic. Emotion makes the prospect take action now, and logic enables them to justify the purchase later.

The key here is to understand what Zig means by the word "emotion." Although an emotion is typically understood to be a feeling such as joy or anger or fear, it is actually much better understood—especially in the context of selling—as an internal motivation.

Fear, for example, is a powerful emotion, but it is also a very powerful motivator. The fear of loss, the fear of failure, the fear of what others think, the fear of the unknown—all are emotions that can be critical motivators in a purchasing decision.

Successful salespeople are keenly aware that a key objective in the sales process is to discover and understand what internal motivations are driving the purchasing decision. If you fail to understand those motivations, you can win the debate but still easily lose the sale.

> **1-on-1 Principle**™
> The prospect's internal motivations (emotions) will always play a role in the buying decision.

*Sadly, the 2012 season didn't end well for Barkley. After starting the 2012 season 6-1, the Trojans lost four of their last five games and then lost in the Sun Bowl to Georgia Tech, 21-7. Barkley injured his shoulder against rival UCLA (a 38-28 loss) and missed the final two games of the year.

CHAPTER 28

THE HAZARDS OF CHANGE

"Progress is a nice word. But change is its motivator.
And change has its enemies."
— ***Robert F. Kennedy***

"No trade will be made unless they want the thing
more than they want their money."
— ***Roy H. Williams***

JIM IS A YOUNG, HARD-CHARGING salesperson. He has gone to work for a relatively new company, one with an exciting new product line. Jim works hard, knows his product line, and is good with customers. Currently, he is working with a prospect who is quite interested in replacing his current product solution.

For good reasons, Jim is excited about this opportunity and has become very enthusiastic about winning the sale. First, his proposed solution has advanced features not currently offered by any of his competitors, which provides him with a tangible performance gap to exploit. Since the prospect has expressed interest in upgrading his current capabilities, Jim feels like he is sitting on the winning hand.

Second, the prospect took Jim aside to let him know his price is a bit high, which Jim takes as a good sign. He assured the prospect that he is willing to be competitive with his pricing and the prospect seemed very pleased. One thing is for sure, Jim isn't going to let this one get away because of price.

Finally, Jim feels very good about the relationship he has developed with the buyer. During his solution presentation, the buyer was very open about the features he likes and had very few objections. From the very beginning, each meeting has been productive, without any hint of resistance.

Jim's competitor in this opportunity is Jennifer, a ten-year industry veteran who represents a much larger and better known company. She has also presented a solid product solution, one that clearly meets all the buyer's requirements, although in comparison to Jim's product, hers is lacking in new features.

As Jim drives to his final meeting with the prospect, he is already spending his commission. He has strong knowledge of Jennifer's product line and, based solely on the merits, he firmly expects to win this sale. He believes that his solution fits the prospect's needs exactly, offers additional features currently unavailable in Jennifer's solution, and price doesn't appear to be an issue. There appears to be nothing in the way of closing this deal.

Imagine Jim's surprise when the prospect welcomes him into his office, thanks him for all of his efforts, and informs him that the company has decided to go with Jennifer's solution. Jim's enthusiasm turns immediately to disbelief, and eventually gives way to anger. How could the prospect choose an inferior product—and at a higher price?

What in the world happened?

IS IT REALLY WORTH IT?

One of the critical issues that prospects struggle with is change. Is the proposed change—to a new product and a new vendor—worth the time and hassle involved in making that change, regardless of the ultimate benefit of the solution?

This is profoundly important for a number of reasons. First, in many sales situations there is a competitor entrenched in the account. Oddly enough, customers will often tolerate less-than-ideal performance from an incumbent vendor simply because of the burdens associated with changing suppliers. Make no mistake, many people do not enjoy change.

Second, while your solution may be full of new, innovative features with significant benefits, in many cases your customers don't want to be a test case. They don't want to endure a number of mistakes while—in the prospect's mind—you work out the kinks in your product.

Finally, if you are a new salesperson, or your company is new to the prospect, you not only have to overcome a natural resistance to change, you also have to overcome the credibility issues associated simply with being new. Your solution may look fantastic, but "new" represents a risk, and risk combined with the hassle of change is often enough motivation to kill a sale.

Always remember that it is not at all uncommon for a prospective customer to tell you that a competitor has a better price or a better offering when, in fact, the real reason they prefer not to move ahead with you is that you, or your company or your product, represent a risk the prospect is not willing to take.

In the prospect's mind, the cost of the change is simply more than the value of the solution you offer.

BETTER ISN'T ALWAYS BETTER

Unfortunately for Jim, the buyer's primary motivation in the scenario above was to make a safe choice—a choice that limited, if not eliminated, any risk to himself for the decision. What Jim didn't know was that this was the buyer's first real test in his new position as purchasing manager and he was quite concerned about making a decision the boss wouldn't criticize.

The buyer was very impressed with Jim's solution, but he didn't want to be among the first to "try out" the new product Jim was offering. He also didn't want to defend a relatively unknown company if something went wrong. So, although Jim presented a seemingly superior solution, his company is smaller and less well-known, and represents a sizeable risk to the buyer in terms of reputation, size, and performance.

Jennifer did something Jim didn't do—she uncovered the buyer's critical motivations and positioned her product and company very carefully to assuage the buyer's concerns. She spent most of her time emphasizing her competitive advantages—flawless delivery, superior after-sale training and support, and a stellar reputation. These benefits completely dispelled the prospect's concerns with risk.

Jennifer won the sale.

Jim went back to the office shaking his head and mumbling something about "stupid customers."

1-on-1 Principle™
Unless a prospect is convinced that the benefits of making a change outweigh the risk associated with it, a sale will not happen.

CHAPTER 29

YOUR FIRST CLOSING ATTEMPT

"What you do have to get, on every call, is a degree of commitment that indicates your time has not been wasted."
— *Stephen Heiman and Robert Miller*

"Unless commitment is made, there are only promises and hopes; but no plans."
— *Peter Drucker*

CERTAIN INDUSTRIES AND CERTAIN types of products allow a sales-person to close a sale in a single sales call. You introduce yourself, gather critical information, move to a presentation of your product or service, handle the prospect's objections, and then work towards closing the deal.

There is plenty to apply in this book if you are a one-call closer, but the reality is that most industries and most products require far more than a single call to complete a deal. In fact, more than one call may be necessary just to complete the discovery process. You may need to meet additional decision makers, complete the qualifying process, learn more about the prospect's current product or service, consult with technical staff, or acquire any number of other critical details.

One of the things I have consistently observed over the years is that if a sales call has progressed well, your prospect will readily set up the next meeting. Many salespeople, however, make a significant mistake in wrapping up a sales call when they fail to close on the next appointment.

Why leave your next appointment to chance? Unless you are making the choice to not pursue the opportunity, the very best way to continue your momentum is to make your first close. Consider ending the call this way:

> "I appreciate your time, Jim. Based on what I've learned to this point, I think there is a pretty strong fit between our companies. If you agree, I would like to pursue the opportunity further. How does that sound?"

Assuming the response to the question above is positive, a very quick and effective technique is to simply ask, "Do you have your calendar in front of you?" Almost without fail, the prospect will reach for a calendar and work with you to set your next meeting time.

CREATING YOUR NEXT STEPS

This is a pivotal point in every sales call, because affirmative action from the prospect indicates a level of engagement in the process. Every sales call, whenever possible, should end with both parties— salesperson and prospect alike—establishing the next steps that need to be completed in order to move the buying process forward.

When the prospect is willing to schedule an appointment, pass on necessary information, introduce you to key people, or in some other way move forward, you can know that you are making progress in the sale. That is why great salespeople always make an effort to set their next appointment at the end of the current call and always attempt to determine the next steps for each party coming out of the call.

On the other hand, I have never seen anyone schedule the next meeting unless they have an interest in moving forward. The sale that is dead in the water typically ends with the prospect saying something like this:

"Leave your brochure and I'll look it over."

"Thanks for stopping by. Why don't you give me some time to think about it."

"I appreciate your time. We'll talk about it and get back to you."

"Do you have some information you can leave?"

In the early years of Monday Night Football, "Dandy Don" Meredith used to signal the end of the game by singing an old Willie Nelson tune. If your prospect uses any of the phrases above, the first words of that song are entirely appropriate for you: "Turn out the lights, the party's over."

1-on-1 Principle™
Setting the next appointment is an easy step that will keep your calendar full, and let you know how engaged your prospect is.

1-on-1 Principles™

Chapter 18:
In selling, interviewing skills are just as important as presentation skills.

Chapter 19:
A salesperson's first objective is to identify and thoroughly qualify high-value, high-probability opportunities.

Chapter 20:
You only get one chance to make a first impression. It can make or break a sale.

Chapter 21:
A clear agenda for the discovery call will set your prospect at ease.

Chapter 22:
An interrogation is the last thing any prospect wants to endure.

Chapter 23:
Getting your prospect talking is the key to unlocking the door to a sale.

Chapter 24:
Knowing which questions to ask is critical. Making them up on the spot is not such a good idea.

Chapter 25:
Don't get ahead of yourself. No credibility means no sale.

Chapter 26:
Performance gaps are a key to creating enthusiastic interest in your product or service.

Chapter 27:

The prospect's internal motivations (emotions) will always play a role in the buying decision.

Chapter 28:

Unless a prospect is convinced that the benefits of making a change outweigh the risk associated with it, a sale will not happen.

Chapter 29:

Setting the next appointment is an easy step that will keep your calendar full, and let you know how engaged your prospect is.

PART VI

PRESENTATION

CHAPTER 30

READY. FIRE! (AIM.)

"Believe passionately in what you do, and never knowingly compromise your standards and values. Act like a true professional, aiming for true excellence, and the money will follow."

— David Maister

"An expert is someone who has succeeded in making decisions and judgments simpler through knowing what to pay attention to and what to ignore."

— Edward de Bono

IN THIS DAY AND AGE, people want what they want—and they want it right now. We have become an impatient society that simply doesn't like to wait.

We want our food fast, and our web browsers even faster. We have microwaves. Self-checkout counters at the grocery store. ATMs. Hertz Gold service (wait in line to rent a car?). We record our favorite shows and fast forward through the commercials.

Kids want their parents' lifestyle right out of college (why wait?). A *60 Minutes* report commented that Millenials, the youngest generation in the current workforce (born between 1980 and 1995), "want to roll into work with their iPods and flip flops around noon, but still be CEO by Friday."

Seriously, in our society, why should you wait for anything? Well, because in sales, rushing ahead is always a mistake.

John "Grizz" Deal, whom I introduced to you in Chapter 23, shares a story that vividly illustrates why rushing through a sale might be a serious mistake:

> I once called up a copier company and was put through to a salesperson. I started to tell him how my copier had died, and before I could say anything else he said he wanted to send me

a packet of information and set up a meeting to talk about their models. I told him he just lost a sale. I had been ready to tell him about my problems, and all he wanted to do was move me through a set sales process.

Note that the salesperson's "set sales process" left out a very important step—discovery. Deal was ready to provide the copier salesperson with all the information that the interview call is designed to uncover, but, instead, the salesperson saw an opportunity and immediately pounced. The prospect obviously needs the product, so move directly to the sales presentation.

But, in moving directly to the sales presentation, salespeople set themselves up for failure and disappointment. In my experience, the quickest way to lose a "sure thing" is to skip a step or, worse, take something for granted.

Unfortunately, this happens way too often. Average salespeople are always looking for shortcuts and easy deals, so they tend to skip the more difficult steps that top salespeople use to consistently create wins.

This can happen in a number of different ways.

A salesperson gets a lead from someone he knows (even a good friend or a family member), and, believing the sale is a done deal, he fails to qualify the opportunity, identify performance gaps, or create a sound value proposition that highlights his competitive advantages. Instead, he rushes into a presentation and leaves the prospect wide open for a skilled professional to do the job right. He often winds up getting his clock cleaned.

Or, a salesperson receives an RFP (request for proposal) or an RFQ (request for quotation or request for qualifications), and immediately treats the request like a well-qualified sales opportunity. Unfortunately, prospects will often solicit bids or quotes in order to filter out vendors, obtain price leverage, or fulfill contracting requirements, so the salesperson spends hours preparing a bid that ultimately results in disappointment.

The challenge here is the same as the previous situation, only worse. Not only does the salesperson fail to qualify the account or identify performance gaps or communicate competitive advantages, he often doesn't even bother to develop a relationship with the prospect. He much prefers to stay in the office and hope for that one-in-a-thousand hit.

Or, a salesperson contacts a prospect who enthusiastically indicates she is quite interested in what the salesperson is selling. The salesperson is then directed to talk to (a very important) someone else—an office manager, an assistant, a buyer, a department manager, or some other gatekeeper. Sensing a great opportunity, the salesperson rushes into a sales presentation with the gatekeeper, but never quite gets the opportunity to follow up with the primary decision maker.

Welcome to your worst nightmare—the opportunity that never seems to materialize, but never seems to quite go away either.

In each of these situations, salespeople allow themselves to be tempted to skip some of the critical steps that create a strong foundation for a win. This is, in fact, what many salespeople substitute for an effective sales process: Get a lead, deliver information, make a sales presentation, close hard, and wait (usually in vain) for a decision.

> **1-on-1 Principle**™
> The quickest way to lose a sale is to skip a step in the sales process.

CHAPTER 31

THE CLASSIC CREDIBILITY BLUNDER

"Boring is the right thought at the wrong time."
— Jack Gardner

"Strategy and timing are the Himalayas of marketing.
Everything else is the Catskills."
— Al Ries

IT SEEMS EVERY COMPANY has a presentation "slide deck" these days—a PowerPoint presentation designed to provide a consistent, standardized corporate presentation for potential customers or vendors. As it turns out, most of these presentations are remarkably similar, regardless of industry. The first several slides outline the company's capabilities, which are followed by a number of slides describing the company's credentials. Or vice versa.

Not long ago, I was reviewing the slide deck presentation of one of my clients in the insurance industry. Predictably, the first slide displayed their corporate logo, but just to make sure the prospect didn't miss the objective of the presentation, the company had added this title to the slide: "Capabilities Presentation."

Clever, huh?

From the customer's perspective, however, this is much like saying, "Here we are, just another company that looks and sounds like every other company." The reality is that when companies are introducing themselves to prospects, it is very much like a beauty pageant. Every salesperson initially presents himself or herself in the very best light, but the customer really learns very little about you except how pretty you are—just like every other contestant.

The downside is that this lack of differentiation, as we discussed previously, inevitably leads to lower prices and compressed margins. Remember, as you introduce yourself and your company for the first time, you are also beginning to answer that critical question, "Why should I buy from you?" Again, the standard answers to this question lead to significant problems, and the use of technology will not change the outcome. The only difference is that when salespeople use a presentation slide deck, those standard answers are generally grouped into two categories—capabilities (We have great quality and service!) and credentials (We are the best in the industry!).

Your capabilities include a description of the following: the company's leadership and workforce, the corporate facilities, manufacturing and/or operations processes, regional locations, specialized technical competencies, logistics, service and support staff, proprietary services, and so forth.

Credentials, on the other hand, are those items that validate the company and its previous work. Credentials include things like industry recognition, licensing or certifications, technical training, vendor relationships, intellectual property, patents, product innovations, and a list of existing and past customers. In some cases, the company's brand and history serve as strong credentials in the marketplace.

Without question, these things will become significant to the customer, but it is important to realize that a great movie doesn't begin with the credits, it ends with them.

STANDING OUT FROM THE CROWD

As important and convincing as your capabilities and credentials may be to your customer at some point, timing is everything in selling. In selling, these two items are much more effectively used as a validation of your company rather than an introduction to the company.

Let me explain.

Just about every other salesperson you compete against will introduce themselves with their company's credentials and capabilities, which, as I suggested, is nothing more than a beauty pageant. It might help distinguish between the pretty girls and the truly beautiful girls, but the reality is the customer still doesn't know much about any of you. In other words, your credentials may legitimize you as a player, but they rarely serve to truly set you apart from your competitors—at a time when your prospect knows very little else about you.

Instead of introducing yourself to prospects by talking about your company and everything that makes it great, you will make a much stronger impression by creating a narrative—a story—that outlines your competitive advantages and presents the important benefits to be gained from working with your company (see Chapters 35 and 36). The dialogue that is sure to follow will surface additional information that will prove quite valuable.

Here is the key: credentials and capabilities make great copy, but they don't make the best headlines. Early in the process, what prospects really want to know is what you can do for them and why they should buy from you. If the introduction to your company looks like every one of your competitors, but with your company name and logo inserted, the only thing you will be talking about soon enough is how much you have to lower your price to get the deal.

On the other hand, if your headline is the powerful answer you have created to answer the question, "Why should I buy from you?" your prospect will want to hear more, and you will still have your company's credentials and capabilities to introduce later—when you have earned some credibility.

Note that some of your capabilities may actually comprise one or more of your competitive advantages—there is absolutely nothing wrong with that. The trap to avoid is the mind-numbing presentation that is focused on the salesperson's company, but provides little or no real insight into the specific ways the prospect can benefit from your products.

Those bells-and-whistles presentations might get high scores for beauty, but there are lots of pretty girls in the contest—and, at this point, you are just another pretty girl.

1-on-1 Principle™

Timing is everything. Your credentials and capabilities will help your credibility, but if you present them in the wrong place, you can easily get lost in the crowd.

CHAPTER 32

AND HERE'S THE PITCH

"Behind every decision the average person makes to buy something
—whether a product or service, your argument or an idea—
is an unspoken emotional motivation."

— Kevin Allen

"Your earning ability today is largely dependent upon your
knowledge, skill, and your ability to combine that
knowledge and skill in such a way that you
contribute value for which customers
are going to pay."

— Brian Tracy

KEVIN ALLEN IS THE LEGENDARY pitch man who is probably best known for leading the team that presented the "Priceless" advertising campaign to MasterCard. This iconic campaign, which debuted during the baseball World Series way back in 1997, has produced over 160 different spots in the past 15 years. It's been marketed in 110 countries, and is among the most well-known and successful ad campaigns of all time.

Here is the original television spot:

"Two tickets: $28."

"Two hot dogs, two popcorns, two sodas: $18."

"One autographed baseball: $45."

"Real conversation with 11-year-old son: Priceless."

"There are some things money can't buy. For everything else, there's MasterCard."

Struggling to gain ground on the market leader (Visa), MasterCard had experimented with five different ad campaigns in the ten years prior to Priceless. There was considerable pressure to produce the right message and the right theme, to "fix the brand," according to recently retired CMO Larry Flanagan. Following a hotly contested competition, MasterCard awarded the business to Allen's team from McCann Erickson.

Reflecting on the decision, Flanagan said McCann Erickson earned the business because they "understood the deep desire of the MasterCard customer, but they understood MasterCard's deep desire, too." This mirrored Allen's perspective, who is convinced that deep desires are critical in every sale:

> Too many pitches are lost because the people undertaking them think—erroneously—that the business matters at hand are the only relevant issue. Deep desires, often unspoken— like the desire to be recognized, to feel appreciated, to create something, to be admired, to lead, to feel safe and secure— are fundamental to any business decision. The business issue and the hidden agenda are intertwined.

Not only do emotions play a role in a buying decision, but, according to Allen, those internal motivations are fundamental to any business decision. This means there are, in fact, two distinctly different agendas that must be discovered and addressed during the sales process.

First there is the business agenda, which contains those items directly relevant to the solution itself. Then, there is a second and even more important agenda—the personal, or, using Allen's words, the hidden agenda. The items on this agenda are not something you will find on an RFQ or RFP or spec sheet or product inquiry. You will have to search out the items on this agenda.

What great salespeople soon discover is the items on the personal (hidden) agenda are fundamental to every sale. They are the internal concerns that motivate the buyer during the decision process. In fact, the key to winning a sale, says Allen, is to "link your leverageable assets to your audience's hidden agenda."

Translation: If you want to consistently win more sales, make sure you understand your prospect's internal motivations, and then link your company's strengths directly to those motivations.

THE PERSONAL (HIDDEN) AGENDA

Consider a hypothetical buyer who manages a department in a medium-sized company. This manager has the responsibility for all the equipment and service contract purchases for the department, and her primary objective is to follow the company's budgetary guidelines while ensuring the company receives the best quality and service available.

This is a very familiar scenario, and it appears that the buying criteria would be fairly straightforward: good quality, excellent service, and, of course, price is extremely critical. However, let's take a closer look at her two agendas and consider how the decision could be influenced by each of them.

The professional agenda outlines "what" the buyer is looking for, and may include one or more of the following:

- To choose the lowest overall price, the lowest lifetime price, or the lowest price per usage

- To improve efficiency

- To lower or eliminate service costs of older products

- To get the best or most innovative feature set

- To get special payment terms

- To obtain additional warranty or maintenance

- To have the product stored, delivered just-in-time, or bundled with other products

- To have immediate access to service or parts

- To obtain product training as a part of the sale

The personal agenda outlines "why" the buyer ultimately makes a decision, and may include any of the following:

- To buy from someone she likes and trusts (enhancing a good relationship)

- To feel important (creating a position of power and/or control)

- To avoid criticism (fear)

- To relieve stress (personal gain)

- To solve someone's complaint or appease someone in particular (personal gain)

- To take the business away from a salesperson she doesn't particularly like (power)

- To look good in front of the boss (to feel valued)

- To get promoted (personal gain)

- To receive a good performance review (to feel valued)

- To enhance her role or status by serving as a technical advisor on the purchase (to feel respected)

- To make more money (personal gain)

Each of these motivations can potentially play a huge role in any given buying decision. In fact, in many cases, the personal motivations will be as strong, if not stronger, than the items on the professional agenda.

Undoubtedly, what the prospect wants to buy is important, but why he or she wants to buy it holds the key to unlocking the most powerful determinants of any purchasing decision. These internal motivations are typically found in the answers to questions like these:

- Why is the prospect considering a change?

- What kinds of difficulties do you anticipate in making a change?

- Is the timing of the purchase important in any way?

- Why would this purchase make sense for the company's long-term business strategies?

- If successfully implemented, what impact would the purchase have on the buyer as an individual?

- How would the buyer be impacted if difficulties were encountered?

Understanding the personal agenda—why the prospect is purchasing—is the key to engaging your prospect on an emotional level and is absolutely critical to winning more sales and defending your margins.

> **1-on-1 Principle™**
> Your presentation may fully address your prospect's solution needs, but you can easily lose the sale if it fails to address your prospect's internal motivations.

CHAPTER 33

No Points for Style

> "Men acquire a particular quality by constantly acting in a particular way."
> — *Aristotle*

> "Success depends upon previous preparation, and without such preparation there is sure to be failure."
> — *Confucius*

ROBERT DENIRO IS CONSIDERED one of the finest actors of his generation. He has starred in some of the classic movies of all time— *The Godfather II, Taxi Driver, Deer Hunter, Raging Bull,* and *The Untouchables.* Like many actors, he wanted to be an actor from a very early age.

DeNiro grew up in Greenwich Village in New York City, launching his eventual career at age ten when he portrayed the Cowardly Lion in a school production of The Wizard of Oz. At 16, he dropped out of high school to enroll in acting classes, and at 31 he added an Academy Award to his resume. The truth is, DeNiro never wanted to do anything else except be on stage.

And many salespeople are exactly the same way.

In the profession of selling, the equivalent to being on stage is making a presentation to a potential customer. It is a chance to put on a show; to dazzle the customer with a brilliant performance. The truth is, many salespeople are convinced they can persuade anyone to buy anything if they can just get in front of a decision-maker. And that is the one place they want to be: on stage, performing.

Certainly, the sales presentation is a critical part of the sales process, but the problem is that many salespeople prefer to skip all the planning, discovery, and preparation stuff and jump right to the main attraction. After all, that is where the magic happens. That is where, allegedly, a prospect is persuaded to make a purchase.

But this is a serious mistake. An effective presentation is far more than just a performance; it is that point in the sales process where a salesperson creates a direct connection between his solution and the personal and professional agendas of the prospect. Done well, that connection leads to a sale. Unfortunately, in my experience, many salespeople, and more than a few sales managers, mistakenly grade a sales presentation more for its special effects than for its actual effectiveness.

For example, there is the animated PowerPoint slide deck complete with multicolor bar graphs and pie charts and eye-popping slide transitions. Or the full-color, 40-page presentation binder full of dazzling graphics, flow charts, and 3-D artist renderings. Or the presentation that includes enough business jargon and industry acronyms to impress a Harvard Business School professor.

Many of these presentations are long on flash and short on what really connects with the prospect.

BIG HAT, NO CATTLE

What does an effective sales presentation really look like? Is it style or substance? Is it critical acclaim, or is it the fact that it results in a signed contract?

My observation is that the effectiveness of a sales presentation is often an impression formed solely from the skills of the presenter: Does the presenter appear confident? Is he or she charismatic? Does the presentation transition smoothly from one slide to the next? Is the slide presentation entertaining? Are the graphics eye-catching?

Consider for a moment what makes for an effective *acting* performance. Is it one that creates critical acclaim or one that makes money?

For DeNiro, that was the question when he turned down a minor role in the original *Godfather* and opted instead to take on a lead role in a movie called *Mean Streets*. The film fared poorly at the box office, but DeNiro received exceptional reviews and won the National Society of Film Critics award for Best Supporting Actor.

So, was his performance effective? Or not? Clearly, it depends on how you define 'effective.' DeNiro made little money in the movie, but the part essentially launched his career and landed him the part of the younger Vito Corleone in *Godfather II*. Which, of course, not only made money but earned DeNiro an Academy Award in 1974.

The same problem exists in sales.

In reality, a slick presentation may look effective but still result in "No Sale." It might look good, sound good, and have people talking about it for days, but if the prospect doesn't buy, was it really effective?

The definition of effective is one thing and one thing only—you win the sale. Think about that. Does anything else really matter? There are no commissions paid for dazzling presentations; the money goes to the salesperson with the signed order. From that perspective, making a dazzling sales presentation and failing to get the order is a bit like the guy who looks like a cowboy but doesn't really deliver the goods.

In Texas, they say it this way: Big Hat, No Cattle. What they mean is, the guy dresses like a cowboy (big hat), but wouldn't know a steer from a steering wheel (no cattle). He looks good, but there is nothing behind the curtain.

Certainly, prospects won't tolerate dull, lifeless presentations, so presentation skills are important. But only up to a point. What the prospect cares about more than style are the answers to these questions: What can you do for me? Do you understand my company? Do you know what we need? Can you address our issues? Do you know what is important to us?

Don't be misled. An effective presentation is one that captures your prospect's interest, addresses the prospect's personal and professional agendas, and differentiates your solution in a way that compels the prospect to want to move forward.

Special effects are optional.

1-on-1 Principle™
An effective sales presentation—one that wins a sale—is much more about preparation than style.

CHAPTER 34

DEAD MONEY

"Information is a source of learning. But, unless it is organized, processed, and available to the right people in a format for decision-making, it is a burden, not a benefit."
— *William Pollard*

"I hate the way people use slide presentations instead of thinking."
— *Steve Jobs*

TEXAS HOLD'EM HAS GAINED enormous popularity in the past dozen years. In 2003, a 28-year-old amateur named Chris Money-maker was the last man standing at the World Series of Poker (WSOP), outlasting a field of 838 players to capture an astounding $2.5 million prize.

The impact of an unknown amateur qualifying in an online tournament and going on to win millions of dollars had a dramatic impact on the game. The very next year, entrants tripled to 2,576. By 2006, over 8,000 players were competing to win a whopping $12 million first-place prize. The vast majority of entrants, like Moneymaker, are amateurs hoping to duplicate his unlikely victory.

'Unlikely' because amateurs don't outplay professional poker players.

In fact, in poker, the term "dead money" is mockingly used to describe novice players who test their luck against the pros. Despite Moneymaker's success, it is generally understood that unskilled players have very little chance against seasoned professionals. Pros believe that completely overmatched amateurs will inevitably leave the game broke; the only thing left to do is figure out who will pocket their chips.

It is important to understand that a very similar scenario exists in the sales profession. Salespeople invest significant amounts of time and energy into sales opportunities not knowing they are the sales equivalent of dead money. Literally, they have no shot at winning the business. Why? Because there are certain mistakes salespeople make over and over in their solution presentations that virtually guarantee failure.

Amateur mistakes.

3 WAYS TO KILL YOUR SALE DEAD

I have seen thousands of sales presentations. Many of them have been tremendously effective. Others, at the opposite end of the spectrum, have been downright painful to watch. Most, however, are neither awful nor extraordinary, they are just average, run-of-the-mill presentations that make the same basic mistakes over and over again. You wouldn't necessarily say they were bad presentations, but they are remarkably ineffective.

The problem is this: the presentation is the point in the sales process where you have to connect your solution directly to the *specific* needs of the prospect. However, there are critical presentation mistakes that a salesperson can make that will typically end any hope of winning the sale.

Here are three common presentation mistakes that guarantee you will not only fail to engage the prospect, but you will waste all the time and energy you've invested in the opportunity. These are three 'dead money' mistakes that amateurs commit over and over again.

1.   PowerPoint Abuse

If you favor PowerPoint for your presentations, the odds of being ineffective increase exponentially. Why? Because PowerPoint is typically used as a one-sided, sit-and-take-notes, no-comments-encouraged, listen-while-I-read-my-slides kind of presentation tool.

An effective sales presentation, on the other hand, is a two-way, ask-questions-and-listen, create-a-productive-dialogue, customer-engagement kind of experience. See the difference? PowerPoint can easily become a crutch, something that is used as a set of presentation notes rather than a visual aid that supports an interactive dialogue with the prospect.

In fact, PowerPoint is so consistently butchered as a presentation tool that it has spawned a common phrase to describe it: 'Death by PowerPoint.' While some people would rather die than speak in public, it is clear that listeners would definitely rather die than listen to another presenter read pages of text from a PowerPoint presentation.

PowerPoint is not only pervasive in the business world, it has also become a standard part of presentations in the military, where it has created its own set of problems:

> Commanders say that behind all the PowerPoint jokes are serious concerns that the program stifles discussion, critical thinking and thoughtful decision-making. Not least, it ties up junior officers—referred to as PowerPoint Rangers—in the daily preparation of slides, be it for a Joint Staff meeting in Washington or for a platoon leader's pre-mission combat briefing in a remote pocket of Afghanistan.
>
> (Bumiller, *New York Times*, April 26, 2010)

Clearly, whether it's used in business or the military—or anywhere else for that matter—the use of PowerPoint limits discussion, isolates listeners, and bores listeners to tears. The question is, can PowerPoint be used effectively in a sales presentation at all?

The answer is 'yes,' but, as the standard warning goes, "Don't try this at home—these are trained professionals." If you are not a trained professional, you should get help immediately, or even consider ditching PowerPoint altogether—this one presentation mistake is surely costing you a lot of money.

If you insist on using PowerPoint (or other similar presentation software) in your presentations, learn how to use it right. Take the time to find an expert who knows how to use PowerPoint effectively. At the very least, read Seth Godin's paper, "Really Bad PowerPoint." Check out *Presentation Zen: Simple Ideas on Presentation Design and Delivery,* by Garr Reynolds. Take the time to study *Beyond Bullet Points* by Cliff Atkinson.

2. Feature Fatigue

Another common mistake that amateurs make is to do the "feature dump" presentation. This presentation style is an encyclopedic approach to revealing a solution to a prospect and is little more than a lengthy recitation of every known feature of your product or service. There is very little in the way of dialogue, just the constant drone of the salesperson.

For prospects, it's like trying to make a purchasing decision after reading a product brochure.

The misstep here is in assuming that when you describe a feature of your product or service, the prospect automatically connects the dots and understands exactly what benefits or impact it will provide. Big mistake.

For example, a prospect can easily become distracted (or, more likely, bored) during your presentation and, as you prattle along, describing feature after feature, fail to register a critical benefit of your solution. As you introduce that one product feature you consider a knock-out punch, the prospect is somewhere else mentally and it doesn't even register.

Another example: You introduce one or more product features you think are most impressive, but they don't impress the prospect quite as you intend. A car salesperson, for instance, boasts that the newest model has 300 horsepower and an exquisite leather interior, thinking power and luxury are big selling points. The prospect, however, is thinking about the price of gas and hot seats in the summer. No thanks.

It is absolutely critical to understand that customers don't buy a product or a service, they buy what the product or service will do for them. They don't buy solutions, they buy solutions to problems.

They don't buy features, they buy results.

3. The Canned Presentation

Finally, there is the "canned" presentation—a standard presentation delivered basically the same way every time. These standard, one-size-fits-all presentations are usually developed by sales managers to ensure that salespeople don't wing it or leave out key selling points.

It is quite common for companies to develop a canned presentation to teach a new salesperson the details of a product or service. Although this isn't a bad approach in teaching new salespeople, the mistake comes when the same presentation is used—exactly as learned—with each and every prospect.

Since a canned presentation is a robotic approach to selling, if salespeople fail to do their homework, they won't address the prospect's specific needs. When you skip planning and discovery, prospects will consider your canned presentation to be a time-waster at best, and mildly insulting at worst.

The real trap in using a canned presentation is that many salespeople believe they can substitute personality or charisma for discovery. They think they can tap dance their way into a sale or mesmerize prospects with their dazzling presentation skills. They have an answer for everything, but those answers typically lack insight into the prospect's specific needs.

Some people like to call this the 'gift of gab,' but that's not what your customers call it. They generally use two letters to describe what you're peddling.

1-on-1 Principle™
Amateur salespeople are successful just often enough to make themselves believe they know what they're doing.

CHAPTER 35

MAKE IT 'STICKY'

"Given the importance of making ideas stick, it's surprising how little
attention is paid to the subject."
— *Chip and Dan Heath*

"The essential difference between emotion and reason is that
emotion leads to action while reason leads to conclusions."
— *Donald Calne, Neurologist, University of British Columbia*

IN 2007, LIBERTY MUTUAL launched a series of television commercials that promoted responsibility: "*Responsibility. What's your policy?*"

Each spot begins with one person observing someone doing something thoughtful for someone else. This, in turn, prompts the observer to act in a similar fashion in the next scene. This happens over and over until the end of the commercial when the narrator says, "When it's people who do the right thing, they call it being responsible. When it's an insurance company, they call it Liberty Mutual."

The commercial implies that you can and should expect your insurer to be responsible. So, do you want to do business with an insurance company that will "do the right thing" or a company that will just collect your premiums?

Of course, Liberty Mutual could have taken the typical approach to television advertising and used the 60-second spot to tout the company's capabilities and credentials: A 100-year-old company. Billions in assets. Agents in every city. A wide range of financial products. Blah, blah, blah.

The difference is that the "responsibility" commercial creates an impression that is memorable. The typical approach does not. The "responsibility" commercial positions the company not as an insurance company, but as a company that will act in the customer's best interests when insurance is needed. The typical commercial, on the other hand, positions the company as just one of many indistinguishable competitors.

What Liberty Mutual is hoping to accomplish with their commercial is exactly what salespeople hope to do in their sales presentations—connect with the customer. You want prospects to feel you understand their situation, that you are speaking directly to their needs, that you get it.

Unfortunately, many sales presentations do everything but connect. They tell about the company. They provide data. They tell you what's wrong with your current product. They offer solutions. But, they fail to truly engage the customer.

How Do You Engage the Customer?

A clue to creating something memorable can be found in the speeches or presentations you've suffered through that are completely forgettable. What do they have in common? The word most commonly used is 'boring,' which is exactly the opposite of connecting. The reality is that two different speakers or presenters can take the exact same material and one can engage the listener while the other puts people to sleep.

Consider the predictable outline that most sales presentations follow:

1. Introduction
2. Company Capabilities and Credentials
3. Summary of Needs
4. Proposed Solution
5. Benefits of Solution
6. Conclusion

If you've seen one, you've seen most all of them—just substitute different company names, different products, and different Power-Point themes. The odds are good that, in taking this all-too-common approach, your company looks and sounds like everyone else, which does little to make you memorable. Worse, however, this approach begs for your solution to be analyzed and dissected and objected to. By default, it fails to engage the customer at an emotional level and, instead, causes an intellectual evaluation of your argument.

In their best-selling book *Made to Stick: Why Some Ideas Survive and Others Die*, Chip and Dan Heath explain this dynamic:

> The problem is that when you hit listeners between the eyes they respond by fighting back. The way you deliver a message to them is a cue to how they should react. If you make an argument, you're implicitly asking them to evaluate your argument—judge it, debate it, criticize it—and then argue back, at least in their minds.

Sounds a whole lot like my early approach to selling that I described in Chapter 27. A presentation is not a debate. We're supposed to be selling, not arguing. But what is the alternative? Chip and Dan Heath provide the answer:

> But with a story…you engage the audience—you are involving people with the idea, asking them to participate with you.

The key to engaging a customer—or any audience, for that matter—is not to present an argument, but to create a narrative or a storyline. Or, to use stories to illustrate key points. Or both. When you can learn how to use a story to communicate your competitive advantages and the key points of your solution, you will be hitting home runs on a regular basis.

"Didn't See That Coming?"

One of my clients did exactly that. The insurance company I mentioned in a previous chapter transformed their stale 'capabilities' presentation into a compelling storyline.

By their own admission, they considered themselves to be in a commoditized industry, offering a commodity product that could be similarly purchased from a number of competitors. Their experience was that price frequently determined the winner and loser in any given opportunity.

The first thing we had to do was discover a competitive advantage. After spending considerable time dissecting their business, they identified not one, but several critical competitive advantages. We took those ideas and rolled them into a narrative about the company, creating a story designed to uniquely position the company and lead prospects to understand how and why they would benefit from choosing them over their competitors.

The key component of their 'story' was actually a television commercial that first aired in 2001. The television spot appears to be an advertisement for a new car, showing a family driving through a scenic neighborhood as an announcer touts the car's exceptional features. At the end of the commercial, the car is suddenly broad-sided in an intersection, and the screen immediately fades to black and displays this message:

"Didn't see that coming?"

"No one ever does."

Originally a Public Service Announcement (PSA), the spot was created by the Ad Council to promote seatbelt usage. My client saw an opportunity to use the idea as an illustration, that the company's real role is to protect its clients from unexpected challenges or risks, and to serve as a level of security that prevents clients from catastrophe. In short, the company is much more than a provider of insurance; it is a partner that protects clients from those situations they would likely never anticipate.

It was absolutely perfect, and the results were immediate and dramatic.

The first time the company used the new approach it was for a presentation to a non-profit Board of Directors. The sales team had concluded the discovery phase of the sales process and reached the point where the Board was ready to dive into the details of the company and its services. From experience, the sales team knew that this was typically the first step in a process that would require additional meetings before any decision was made.

At the conclusion of the presentation, the team answered a number of questions from board members, but, instead of being thanked and dismissed, they were asked to wait outside while the board continued discussions. Not long afterward, the team was invited back into the meeting and, much to their surprise, they were awarded the business on the spot!

A coincidence? Not at all. They discovered what was important to the prospect and connected their competitive advantages directly to those needs through a powerful narrative. The level of engagement with the prospect was outstanding.

As any great storyteller will tell you, the power of stories is remarkable. They not only capture your listeners' interest, but, as *Made to Stick* points out, they prompt them to act:

> The story's power, then, is twofold: It provides simulation (knowledge about how to act) and inspiration (motivation to act). Note that both benefits, simulation and inspiration, are geared to generating action . . . .

> A credible idea makes people believe. An emotional idea makes people care . . . the right stories make people act.

When you tell a story effectively, you not only engage the listener, but, if that story effectively addresses the prospect's needs, you compel them to act.

> **1-on-1 Principle™**
> 'Sticky' presentations are not only memorable, they compel your prospect to act.

CHAPTER 36

CREATE AN IMPRESSION

"Steve Jobs does not sell computers; he sells an experience."
— **Carmine Gallo, author of The Presentation Secrets of Steve Jobs**

"Persuasion is not about getting people to see things your way;
it's about getting them to see your point in their way."
— **Jack Malcolm** *

THE LATE STEVE JOBS had the legendary ability to challenge and in-spire. An acknowledged master at captivating an audience, his new product announcements at Apple were a must-see event—as much for Jobs' presentations as the introduction of yet another block-buster, market-changing iProduct.

He masterfully used stories and illustrations to make critical points or help listeners appreciate his viewpoint. For example, in a 2003 CBS *60 Minutes* interview, he used this interesting metaphor to describe one of his core perspectives on business:

> My model of business is the Beatles. They were four very tal-ented guys who kept each other's kind of negative tendencies in check. They balanced each other, and the total was greater than the sum of the parts. That's how I see business. Great things in business are never done by one person. They're done by a team of people.

The Beatles as a business model. Not something you would likely forget, and he knew that.

While stories were a critical aspect of his presentations, he also had a natural flair for the dramatic. In 1987, as he was recruiting, John Sculley, then CEO of Pepsi, to join Apple, Jobs asked, "Do you want to spend the rest of your life selling sugared water, or do you want a chance to change the world?" Two decades later, he introduced the iPhone to the world at the 2007 Macworld Expo with these words: "We're going to make history together today."

As a presenter, Jobs had the extraordinary ability to capture an audience and lead them inescapably to a climactic ending.

For salespeople, there is much to learn from Jobs' style and his approach to presentations. However, it is critical that salespeople realize one significant difference between Jobs' presentations and a *sales* presentation. Salespeople must necessarily create a dialogue with the prospect, soliciting input and agreement as they work through their solutions. The sales presentation is not entertainment or a simple announcement; it is the introduction of your solution in a way that is designed to compel your prospect to a decision in your favor.

THREE STEPS TO BLOCKBUSTER SALES PRESENTATIONS

A great presentation, first and foremost, requires a lot of thought and preparation. Successful sales professionals do not wing it, and they don't leave things to chance. Instead, they combine three of the concepts we have discussed in previous chapters to create a blockbuster sales presentation—every time. Here are the three critical pieces:

1. Relevant content.

2. Customer involvement.

3. A compelling narrative.

Content comes from the discovery phase of the sales process. Involvement is created when salespeople know which questions to ask, and why. A narrative is an approach to delivering the content of the solution in a way that is memorable, and, more importantly, prompts a purchasing decision.

1. Create great content.

Great content is content that it is relevant to each individual prospect. It seizes the prospect's attention not just because you are a skilled presenter, but because it directly addresses your prospect's personal and professional agendas.

Strong content is not only relevant, it is compelling. This is where the first two phases of the sales process pay huge dividends. Salespeople who have researched the prospect's company, understand specific needs, and have valuable ideas to offer have tremendous credibility.

That means 'winging it' is not an option. Do your homework. Find out everything you can about your prospect's business: how they compete, how they go to market, what their business goals are, what challenges they face and so on. With the tools that are readily available today, there is very little you can't know about your prospect, and once you complete your research, you will be amazed how often the correct approach to that account becomes crystal clear.

Once you realize how you want to approach the prospect, write a clear and concise theme for the presentation that will serve as a guide for developing those key points you want to emphasize. Jack Malcolm, an award-winning speaker and presenter, and author of *Strategic Sales Presentations*, offers this insight:

> You should write a clear theme because it is the most important step in creating an exceptional presentation.
>
> As obvious as it may sound, you have to be absolutely crystal clear in your own mind about what you want your listeners to take away from your presentation. That becomes your overriding theme.
>
> Your theme provides focus, which infuses your presentation with purpose, clarity, and power. It also saves time in the preparation and in the delivery of the talk.

The bottom line is this: you want your listeners to be perfectly clear about what you want them to do and why they should to do it. If you aren't clear, why should they be?

Always remember: great content—the *right* content—is critical in a superior presentation. Discovering that content takes research, and presenting it well means you need clarity about the theme of your presentation.

2. Create customer involvement.

In prior chapters, I have encouraged you to think carefully about each interaction with the prospect, to consider what questions will create engagement and interactive dialogue. The solution presentation is no different. As you move through the presentation, it is important to further involve your prospect.

An effective way to create involvement early in the presentation is to confirm your understanding of critical aspects of the personal or professional agendas. One simple question will often suffice to create interaction:

"My understanding is [*whatever you want to confirm*]. Is that correct?"

This question is a good one because it can easily lead to further dialogue about the specific issue, but it is also important for another reason: things can change during the course of the buying process. The very best salespeople ensure they have the most current information about anything that may be central to the solution presentation, particularly when the data was acquired very early in the sales process.

On the off chance your prospect may simply answer 'yes' or 'no' to your question above, you should have a follow-up question prepared—a relevant question that will continue the discussion. Here are examples:

"How does that affect your budget (or some other issue)?"

"What will that mean to the company in the long-term?"

"What impact would this have on your team/department?"

The point is that a well-designed presentation is one that uses strategic questions to place your prospect directly into the presentation's dialogue. Successful salespeople clearly understand one very important sales principle: the more your prospect talks, the more information you have to use.

3. Create a story.

Like Steve Jobs, skillful presenters take the content they develop and weave that information into a narrative—a story—that is compelling to the customer. The narrative is designed to take listeners on a journey, to engage them at both an emotional and intellectual level.

In many cases, the narrative may be as simple as using a series of analogies or illustrations to make key points as you go along, but make no mistake, a good storyline is the key to engaging your prospect. Not just any story, but one that creates interest, that produces an emotional response. Peter Gruber, film producer, corporate executive, and author of the outstanding book, *Tell to Win: Connect, Persuade, and Triumph with the Hidden Power of Story*, explains:

> Anybody who's ever read a novel or watched a movie knows that a story that fails to deliver surprise is dead on arrival. The same rule holds for stories told in person to business audiences. The shock value may be as subtle as a shrug or a pang of regret. Not every story needs thrills and chills, but without some surprise, you'll lose your listener's attention.

Not surprisingly, Gruber's book is full of great stories, stories that capture your imagination and vividly illustrate critical points with perfect clarity. Don't lose sight of your objective—the idea is not to tell a story just to tell a story, but to craft your message inside of a narrative that captures the customer's attention. Gruber offers this simple, yet powerful template for doing just that:

- First...get your listeners' attention with an unexpected challenge or question.

- Next...give your listeners an emotional experience by narrating the struggle to overcome that challenge or to find the answer to the opening question.

- Finally...galvanize your listeners' response with an eye-opening resolution that calls *them* to action.

The power of storytelling cannot be overstated as the means to more consistent sales success. More importantly, it is a key in differentiating your solution from every other competitor's solution—something that becomes enormously helpful when it's time to negotiate price.

1-on-1 Principle™
Powerful questions and great stories are the keys to creating a compelling presentation.

*For much more detailed insight on creating world-class sales presentations, make sure to read Jack Malcolm's excellent book, *Strategic Sales Presentations*, available on Amazon and at www.jackmalcolm.com.

CHAPTER 37

REACHING THE FINISH LINE

"The harder the conflict, the more glorious the triumph."
— *Thomas Paine*

"Remember, you cannot make anyone change his or her mind.
You can only give them new information
to make a new decision."
— *Zig Ziglar*

NOW THAT THE FORMAL presentation is over, it's time to 'handle' objections and 'close' the sale. At least that's the way I was taught when I started years ago: find a need, make a presentation, handle the objections, ask for the sale.

To that end, Zig Ziglar wrote one of the all-time classic sales books on how to get to the finish line: *Secrets of Closing the Sale*. I was just a few years into my career when Zig's book was released in 1985, and I wore out a couple of copies learning how to deal with objections and lead buyers to a positive decision.

It's important to note, however, that Zig's background was selling cookware door-to-door, and much of his perspective was based on meeting a prospect and reaching a decision in a single call. Although there are notable exceptions, for most salespeople the transactions in business-to-business selling (B2B) are not one-call close propositions.*

The truth is that many of the early prominent sales trainers were from industries like real estate (J. Douglas Edwards and Tom Hopkins), insurance (Frank Bettger and W. Clement Stone) , and door-to-door product sales (Dale Carnegie and Zig Ziglar). Selling in these industries required strong one-call closing skills because the salesperson quite often didn't get a second chance. They did not typically make multiple calls, gather information, and build relationships. Instead, these sales pros, in a single call, would discover a need, make a presentation, handle objections, and then attempt—usually several times—to close the deal.

I have not worked in one-call close industries. My experience in closing sales is quite different. I have consistently found that when I followed the sales process carefully and involved the prospect all along the way, closing the deal was often as simple as asking this question:

"Is there any reason you wouldn't want to move forward?"

But, that was only if I actually had to *ask* a question. It is not at all unusual, when you've done your homework well and connected solidly with the prospect, to hear the prospect say, "This looks great. What's the next step?"

As I write this chapter, it has happened twice in the past week. A prospect has asked me, "What's the next step?" Ready to proceed, they want to know how the process will go forward. Sure, there may still be some details to resolve, but the prospect is seriously engaged and the finish line is in sight.

That being said, I can sense your skepticism. No, I obviously don't win every sale. Nor am I suggesting that selling is so easy that some preparation and a dazzling presentation will win every sale.

There are, in fact, many reasons why we don't win, even when we do everything very, very well. However, my experience is that when I have strong credibility and I have done my job well, a prospect is typically forthcoming about where we stand, one way or the other.

In either case, rarely, if ever, will a series of tricky closing questions make a difference in closing the deal. There might yet be objections to resolve and there might be further negotiations to work through, but when you have done your job well, handling your prospect's objections is a straightforward process—either you can re-solve the issue(s) or you can't.

That means there will be times when your prospect seems to be at an impasse. They leave the impression that they are unsure about something, or they appear to have some doubts or questions, or they appear as if they don't know how they are going to proceed. In those instances, ask one of the following questions:

"Is there anything critical that I have failed to address?"

"What concerns do you have at this point?"

"My sense is there may be an issue or two we need to discuss. Is that right?"

Again, when you've developed a good relationship with the prospect and they've been involved in the presentation, they will typically be forthcoming about the challenges they see with your solution.

Don't get me wrong. I am not suggesting you don't need to read *Secrets of Closing the Sale*. Quite the contrary! What I am saying, however, is that I am amazed at how often professional salespeople win a sale after simply working out a few details on how to get started. Buyers who are genuinely engaged will often initiate the close, even if their first (or only) objection is designed to negotiate your price (more on price issues in Chapter 47).

1-on-1 Principle™
It's much easier to handle objections and close a sale when the prospect is fully engaged.

---

*For tremendous insight into the world of one-call closing, please see Robert Terson's excellent book, *Selling Fearlessly: A Master Salesman's Secrets for the One-Call Close Salesperson,* available on Amazon and at www.sellingfearlessly.com.

CHAPTER 38

NO PLACE LIKE HOME

"Entrepreneurs are simply those who understand that there is little difference between obstacle and opportunity and are able to turn both to their advantage."

— Niccolo Machiavelli

"Often the difference between a successful person and a failure is not [that] one has better abilities or ideas, but the courage that one has to bet on one's ideas, to take a calculated risk—and to act."

— Andre Malraux

IN 2012, ESPN FILMS released a *30-for-30* documentary entitled, *There's No Place Like Home*. The film chronicled the sale of the "Founding Rules of Basketball," the thirteen original rules of basketball created by Dr. James Naismith in 1891. To many, this historical document—two pages typed and signed by Dr. Naismith—is perhaps the most noteworthy piece of sports memorabilia ever.

Josh Swade, a former Kansas University student, had become aware in early 2010 that Naismith's rules were going to auction. Swade works for a media production company in New York City; he is also a self-described Kansas Jayhawks basketball fanatic. Possessed of a keen understanding of basketball history and the significance of Naismith's rules to Kansas basketball, in particular, Swade embarked on a personal quest to bring the rules to Kansas and to create a film documenting the story.

Naismith founded the University of Kansas basketball program just a few years after publishing his rules, and he would coach there for nine seasons. One of his players was three-time letterman, Forrest Clare "Phog" Allen, who would eventually become the Jayhawks second head basketball coach. In 39 years as the Kansas coach, Allen tallied 590 wins and won three national titles.

He also coached two basketball legends—Dean Smith and Adolph Rupp.

Smith and Rupp posted 879 and 876 victories at North Carolina and Kentucky, respectively, making them the fourth and sixth most successful coaches in NCAA basketball history. Those three basketball programs—Kansas, North Carolina, and Kentucky—are currently the three most successful schools in NCAA basketball history, and all are linked to Dr. James Naismith, the founder of basketball.

For Swade, the *only* place those rules could wind up was in Lawrence, Kansas, the fountainhead of basketball. The challenge, however, was money. Lots of money. The rules were projected to sell for well over $1 million. So, Swade began his quest to bring Naismith's rules to Kansas by contacting the most prominent benefactors of Jayhawks basketball.

Ultimately, he scheduled appointments—and presentations—with three prominent donors to the program.

His first presentation, just 20 days before the auction, was a miserable failure. The 'prospect,' with little idea of Swade's intentions, looked very uncomfortable and showed little interest in the idea of donating funds to purchase the document. Swade asked few questions, made a very poor presentation, and ultimately tried to close (weakly) by asking, "What do you think of that?"

As it turns out, he didn't think much of it at all.

Swade's second presentation was a little better. He had the benefit of additional exposure on a sports radio show, so the prospect was a little more aware of his objectives. He did not, however, appear any less uncomfortable.

He began with a couple of questions: "When I say 'Kansas basketball', what comes to mind?" and "What do you love about Kansas basketball?," but he never really created any engagement with the prospect. Sensing his prospect's discomfort, Swade said, "I'm not here to put you on the spot," but he tried to close the deal by asking, "I'm out here asking for your help. What are your thoughts?"

Answer? "I'd have to discuss it with my wife."

Swade was learning fast. With time running out and only one solid prospect left, he realized he needed to make serious changes to have any hope of success. His passion for Jayhawks basketball was readily apparent, but he was failing to translate that passion into anything a prospect would act on.

His final prospect was David Booth, a successful businessman who had grown up less than a mile from Allen Field House and graduated from Kansas University. In 2004, Booth and his wife Suzanne had donated $9 million to the university to build the Booth Family Hall of Athletics, which was attached to Allen Field House.

In preparation for his meeting with Booth, Swade created a short film clip that featured a number of former Jayhawks coaches and players, including Roy Williams and Larry Brown (two of only eight coaches in KU's 139-year history), and Danny Manning (led the Jayhawks to a national title under Larry Brown in '87-88). Also featured in the video clip was Jay Bilas, an ESPN basketball analyst and a former Duke University basketball player.

In the video, each of these prominent basketball figures (and several others) was asked their opinion about where the rules 'belonged.' Each had the same answer: Kansas University.

THE FINAL PRESENTATION

Swade began his presentation by inquiring about Booth's memories growing up just down the road from Allen Field House. After a short dialogue, he cued the video, which included these two powerful sound bites:

> Larry Brown: "I wish the rules of the game would be there [at Kansas University] on display, and hopefully somebody will step up and keep those simple rules at the University."

> Roy Williams: "There's no question in my mind, I'd like to see 'em back at the University of Kansas. For 15 years,

Kansas basketball felt like home. For those rules to be in that museum, in that Hall of Fame, at Allen Field House, on Naismith Drive, that's where I think they should be."

As the video concluded, you could sense Booth's complete connection to the task at hand. Swade had created an emotional bond between Kansas University, Naismith's rules, influential coaches and players, and Booth himself.

Booth (as the video ends): "It is the right place for it."

Swade: "We gotta get these rules—we gotta get these home."

Booth (agreeing): "We gotta get 'em home."

Whenever salespeople build a compelling story and create an emotional connection, sales just have a tendency to close themselves. And so it was in this case. Without further prompting or further questions, Booth said, "Let me cut to it. I'll be happy to be a lead sponsor in this project. I'll do more than my fair share to get this thing done."

On December 10, 2011, David and Suzanne Booth purchased Naismith's Founding Rules of Basketball for a record $4.3 million and donated the document to Kansas University.

1-on-1 Principle™
Closing a deal seems effortless when you create a compelling story.

1-on-1 Principles™

Chapter 30:
The quickest way to lose a sale is to skip a step in the sales process.

Chapter 31:
Timing is everything. Your credentials and capabilities will help your credibility, but if you present them in the wrong place, you can easily get lost in the crowd.

Chapter 32:
Your presentation may fully address your prospect's solution needs, but you can easily lose the sale if it fails to address your prospect's internal motivations.

Chapter 33:
An effective sales presentation—one that wins a sale—is much more about preparation than style.

Chapter 34:
Amateur salespeople are successful just often enough to make themselves believe they know what they're doing.

Chapter 35:
'Sticky' presentations are not only memorable, they compel your prospect to act.

Chapter 36:
Powerful questions and great stories are the keys to creating a compelling presentation.

Chapter 37:
It's much easier to handle objections and close a sale when the prospect is fully engaged.

Chapter 38:

Closing a deal seems effortless when you create a compelling story.

PART VII

DELIVERY

CHAPTER 39

DELIVER THE GOODS

"Profit in business comes from repeat customers, customers that boast about your project or service, and that brings friends with them."

— W. Edwards Deming

"Never assume something you can check. Pay attention to the details. Roll up your sleeves and get your hands dirty. If the project is important, every single detail is important."

— Jeffrey J. Fox, author of How to Become a Rainmaker

I WAS CLOSE TO FINISHING UP lunch one day at an Arby's restaurant when an employee came slipping and sliding out from behind the counter clutching a single, foil-wrapped sandwich in his hand. "He didn't get his whole order," he exclaimed loud enough for even the most disinterested patron to hear, and he practically bounced out the side door in pursuit of his last customer.

The table where I sat afforded me a view of the front counter, and I was also positioned next to an outside window where I could see drive-in customers stop and pick up their orders. I watched the young man track down the customer and deliver the balance of his order, and when he popped back in the door, he had a satisfied smile on his face.

As this vignette unfolded, the Assistant Manager wandered out from behind the counter, and I caught her rolling her eyes. Noticing another employee cleaning a table in the seating area close to me, she stepped over and offered up this pearl of wisdom: "Can you believe that?" she asked with a smirk. "He took that sandwich out there and didn't even put it in a bag."

No bag? Inexcusable.

The manager seemed quite intent on pointing out the young man's shortcomings, and when he returned she didn't bother to praise his initiative, or thank him for the effort, or offer any appreciation for going the extra mile. Instead, she criticized him publicly for failing to put the sandwich in a bag.

Seriously? *"How about a little something, you know, for the effort?"*

Here's the kicker. I've been through that situation as a customer on more than one occasion at that very restaurant (clearly, I'm a little slow on the uptake). I've driven away, arrived at home, and discovered the bad news—an incomplete order. In fact, this happens so often in the fast-food industry that marketers have discovered a "third window" at fast-food places: a window to collect your money, a window to get your order, and a third, imaginary "window" where customers stop to make sure they received everything they ordered.*

The point here is that customers expect to get what they paid for. Customers expect you to deliver the goods. Most importantly, they expect any challenges that may arise to be rapidly resolved. So, here is a motivated, enthusiastic restaurant employee, ready and willing to deliver on that very simple idea and the manager is completely oblivious to how important his actions were. Instead, she disparages the poor guy in front of customers and fellow employees.

Which means, of course, that the next time I drive through and my order is short, I probably won't have to worry about this guy running me down with the missing sandwich.

"So, I got that goin' for me."

KEYS TO SUCCESSFUL IMPLEMENTATION

Professional salespeople understand that once a sale is won, the real work has only just begun. Once you have an order, your customer will have very high expectations for the implementation of your product or service. Customers not only want what they pay for, they quite often expect and demand perfection. Or better.

What customers often experience, however, are salespeople who go missing during the implementation phase of the sales process. Salespeople can be hard to reach, slow to respond, and in many cases, much too busy with the next opportunity to ensure things go as promised. In an era where every blunder, every mix-up, and every lapse in judgment can be highlighted in a variety of social media applications, this is a mistake of considerable proportions.

For you to be consistently successful, you need to buy into the idea that your customers want a salesperson who is both *accessible* and *responsive*. Customers want a partner who will make sure the implementation of the solution proceeds exactly according to plan. More than anything, customers want someone who, rather than sticking his or her head in the sand, will gladly tackle any challenges that may arise.

To meet and exceed these expectations, and to elevate your credibility to the status of Trusted Advisor, you need to DELIVER. You need to pay attention to the details. You need to do the things that will set you apart from the myriad of mediocre salespeople you compete against.

1. Create a Checklist

First, create a very simple tool that will guide your customers through the implementation of your product or service. Provide your customer with a checklist of the key aspects of the implementation process—delivery dates, personnel involved, steps to completion, and so forth. Be sure to include contact information for any and all personnel who will be involved.

Keep a copy for yourself, and check regularly to ensure that implementation is going exactly as planned.

2. Inform the Key Players

Next, clarify with your customer which individuals in the company will be directly or indirectly impacted by the installation and/or implementation of your solution. You probably have this list compiled as a part of your discovery research, but review and revise it as necessary. It should include anyone and everyone impacted by any changes your solution creates, including end-users, order entry, accounting, inventory management, shipping and receiving, technical support, and any number of other departments.

Once you know who will be impacted by the implementation of your product or service, you can create a timeline and methodology for proactively communicating with them to ensure a smooth transition process. Make sure everyone on that list knows exactly how to contact you.

3.   Stay Involved

Many products and services require some form of training or orientation. This aspect of implementation is an area where you can really set yourself apart from the competition.

There is a significant difference between customers who receive training and customers who acquire *confidence* in your product or service as a result of your training. You not only need to ensure that relevant personnel receive the appropriate training, you also need to pay very close attention to how well the training progresses.

Comments offered by end-users, both good and bad, are absolutely invaluable to you and your company, and you want to be acutely aware of any critics of your product or service. Acknowledging and dealing with specific issues that may arise will pay enormous dividends for future business opportunities or potential referrals. Keep in mind that, with few exceptions, companies understand that implementation is rarely, if ever, flawless. The critical factor for customers—and what distinguishes between good and bad salespeople—is how those situations are resolved.

The side benefit of your continued involvement in the implementation phase of the sales process is the opportunity to further build your relationship with the buyer, and to create additional relationships that will strengthen your overall credibility within the account.

YOU ARE THE COMPANY

The quickest way to create a poor impression of you is to fail to deliver the one thing your customer needs most—your attention. Let's be clear: In the eyes of your customers, YOU are responsible for making sure they get exactly what they purchased. YOU are accountable for making certain that implementation of your product or service is completed successfully. The blame for poor communication, flawed implementation, or a failure to quickly and successfully resolve issues will be placed squarely on your shoulders.

Future sales are often sacrificed because the delivery of the solution is rife with minor issues and poor communication that quickly erodes the trust you have worked so hard to develop. This can largely be avoided by simply overseeing the process and being proactive in communicating with the customer. The payoff is enormous when customers observe that you are someone who takes care of business.

Take note: if you typically hand off implementation of your product/service to a technical support team, make it clear to the customer that you are always available and you will personally resolve any issues that arise.

1-on-1 Principle™
YOU are the company. YOU are responsible. Make sure it happens the way YOU said it would.

---

*Many thanks to Dr. Steven Greene, Dean of the College of Business at Oral Roberts University, who shared this insight in his presentation to a group of business executives in 2012.

CHAPTER 40

LEVERAGE YOUR SUCCESS

"To achieve radically better sales results, you must become radically more valuable to customers—*strategically* valuable."
— *Mark Miller, author of A Seat at the Table*

"Little things make the difference. Everyone is well prepared in the big things, but only the winners perfect the little things."
— *Paul "Bear" Bryant*

WOULDN'T IT BE GREAT to know the single biggest factor that informs or influences a buyer's purchasing decision? Your objective during the discovery phase of the sales process is to find those critical motivations that drive your customer's buying decision, but wouldn't it be a huge advantage if you knew there was one primary factor that, more than all the others, influenced your customer's buying behavior?

It seems like a pipe dream. After all, in any given purchasing scenario, who knows what factors, or combination of factors, will impact a buying decision?

But what if we considered just four important variables that play a role in a buyer's decision-making process? Try it for yourself. Given the following four variables, decide how much you think each of them contribute, on average, to the buyer's final decision (divide by percentage, all four to total 100 percent) :

- Price of the Solution   _____
- Quality of the Solution   _____
- A Total solution   _____
- Effectiveness of the salesperson   _____

Which one do you think is typically *most* important to a customer?

If we listen to our customers at all, we would probably think price is far and away the most important. Fortunately, we don't have to guess. HR Chally (www.chally.com), a "global leadership and sales potential and performance measurement firm," has the answer. Using data collected from 80,000 business customers over the course of 14 years, company researchers determined that, of the four variables listed above, the *effectiveness of the salesperson* is the single most important factor in a customer's buying decision.

You read that right. You, the salesperson, are ultimately more important to the final decision than the actual product or service, the quality of that product or service, or the price of that product or service!

Here is the breakdown:

1. Salesperson effectiveness—39 percent.

2. The availability of a total solution—22 percent.

3. Quality—21 percent.

4. Price—18 percent.

Four critical items, to be sure. Each with a part to play in influencing the customer's decision. However, according to HR Chally, the most significant influence on a buyer's final decision is your effectiveness as a salesperson.

Is price important? Certainly. But not quite as important as salespeople think. In fact, according to this data, we can easily conclude that the salesperson is more than twice as important in determining a buying decision as price! And, although salespeople tout the importance of product quality (for good reason), it still isn't as important as you are. Taken together, quality and price *combined*— according to 80,000 buyers—are only as important as the salesperson!

Get the picture? This is an absolutely critical point to understand: you can have the right product, outstanding quality, and a competitive price, and you are still only about 60% of the way to a win!

The difference maker? You, the salesperson.

How to Make a Difference

Learning how to make a difference in your customers' decisions is as simple as thinking about what we disdain in salespeople. As customers ourselves, we dislike salespeople who are pushy, disrespectful, arrogant, and concerned only about making a sale. We hate it when salespeople are slow to respond, unwilling to help, or seemingly disinterested in dealing with problems. What we want is a salesperson who is available, supportive, and invested in our success—both during and after the sale.

That is what makes you so important. Think about it: you go to a great restaurant where the food is great but the service is terrible—what is your response? The product is good, the price is acceptable, but the salesperson (the waiter) is a failure. How does that impact you? Typically, no matter how good the food, the lasting impression will be a negative one because the experience was poor.

This simple example should make it very clear why the salesperson is critical to the buying decision and lead you to understand exactly what you need to do to make a difference.

1. Always Make Good on Your Promises

This is the big problem in the restaurant example. There is the implied promise that you will receive good service. When that doesn't happen, the entire experience is compromised. You simply cannot fail to keep your promises. Although this should be self-evident to any salesperson, it is a very common failure.

No matter how small the detail, when you promise, you must deliver. I understand it is difficult, if not impossible, to be perfect, but early on in your relationship, you simply cannot afford to miss something you have promised to the customer. As you develop a stronger relationship with your customer, your credibility won't be impacted by a small mistake, but early on it is critical that you deliver.

Too many times I have promised something to someone in passing, and then completely forgotten ten minutes later. Sometimes, I can get so many things going at once, I forget a small but important detail. You don't do that too many times before the customer is giving you an ear full. Or, worse, they just quit buying.

I eventually made it a habit to write down whatever I promised to do. I carried a notebook or a planner, and I wrote things down. With the tools available today, it gets easier and easier to capture the small details and deliver exactly what you promise.

2. Be Accessible

You cannot overestimate how important it is to be accessible to your customer, especially during the implementation phase of the sales process. After a sale is made, inept salespeople take longer to return calls, reply to inquiries, and deal with issues. Which, by the way, from the customers' perspective, is tantamount to saying, "All I really care about is my commission."

Understand your customers' expectations. If a customer expects a one-hour response time, you need to know that and prepare for it, or change the expectation. In many cases you can set priorities based on communication type. For instance, you may agree to answer an email by the end of the day, but respond to a voice mail within one to two hours. You might use text messaging as an 'emergency only' type of communication, or use it as your primary mode of contact.

The main thing is to get on the same page. Give your customer two or three ways to contact you. In some cases, you may want to provide an emergency back-up contact in case you are temporarily unavailable due to travel or other circumstances.

3. Own the Results

It's hard to imagine, but many salespeople actually run away from customer problems. The reasons vary, but salespeople often go missing-in-action when things go awry. However, as clichéd as it may sound, some of the very best business relationships are forged through adversity. Customers often judge a salesperson not on what they do right, but in the way in which they handle those things that go wrong.

One consistent mistake that salespeople are prone to make is blaming someone else in the company—the shipping department, or accounting, for example—when something goes wrong. Remember, YOU are the company. Regardless of who may actually be at fault, if you blame others, the customer will perceive that you don't care enough to be accountable for the solution you so enthusiastically sold them.

Take responsibility, handle the problem, and ensure the customer is satisfied. It doesn't matter where the fault may lie; what the customer will see is that you are willing to take care of business.

Your credibility, and their trust in you, will increase dramatically.

4. Be Humble

First, never forget the two most important words you know: "Thank you." Gratitude is grossly underappreciated as a powerful means of influence, and it is shocking how often salespeople fail to show appreciation for the business they win. Although customers exchange funds for your product or services, an expression of appreciation for their business will help strengthen the business relationship.

Make sure to say, "Thanks for your business" or "I appreciate the opportunity to work with you," each and every time you win a sale. You can express your gratitude in an email message. You can say thank you in person. Or, if you really want to make an impression, you can send a personal, handwritten card. The one thing you can never do is say thank you too much.

Second, never forget the people in the background. Salespeople often get focused on the person (or people) at the top—the owner, the CEO, the General Manager, the department head, the executive team, or whomever—and they forget or ignore the many others who can easily influence those same people. Always make it a point to be polite and respectful to receptionists, assistants, and other support people. Engage those employees that you meet. Take time with those individuals who have questions or express an interest in what you're doing. Many, many opportunities have been lost because someone with influence developed a negative impression of a salesperson who seemed arrogant or uncaring.

> **1-on-1 Principle**™
> You can leverage your success by providing the extraordinary service and support that customers crave.

1-on-1 Principles™

Chapter 39:

YOU are the company. YOU are responsible. Make sure it happens the way YOU said it would.

Chapter 40:

You can leverage your success by providing the extraordinary service and support that customers crave.

PART VIII

SUCCESS HABITS

CHAPTER 41

PERSONAL MARKETING

"The price of excellence is discipline. The cost of mediocrity is disappointment."

— William Arthur Ward

"More customer service hopes have been wrecked on the rigid shores of immobile bureaucratic minds than anywhere else."

— Ken Blanchard, author of From Raving Fans:
A Revolutionary Approach to Customer Service

I'M NOT SURE IF IT was *Holmes on Homes* or *The Property Brothers*, but at some point in time, cable television managed to convince me I might like to flip a house.

As if I have the first idea.

"Flipping" a house, for all intents and purposes, seems like a simple idea: purchase an old or run-down residential property, do a complete makeover, and resell it for a big profit. A 30-minute reality show really makes it look easy—until you watch someone who has no idea what they are doing try to pull it off. Inevitably, the unskilled, the uninformed, and the unprepared crash and burn.

However, not to be deterred by rational thinking—and reinforcing the notion that people don't make decisions logically—I noticed a foreclosure property not far from my own residence and decided I was ready to join the ranks of the crash-and-burn crowd.

Locating the property online, I found a number for the Listing Agent and gave her a call. I had called during the evening hours, so I was privileged to reach an answering service. The gentleman could not locate the name of the listing agent in his contact list, but assured me he would pass my message along.

About two hours later, I finally got a call. As promised, the answering service had reached the agency and one of the agents had been notified of my inquiry. As I learned just moments later, she was calling from a restaurant.

"Is this Kelly?" she hollered amidst the background noise.

"Yes, it is."

"I got a text."

"OK."

No, that's all she said: "I got a text." Like I should know who it was and why she might be calling. But, after a couple of questions back and forth, we finally figured out who we were and why we were calling each other, and we got down to business.

Actually, although she had called *me*, I felt like I was interrupting her dinner. But, like any other annoying customer, I pressed ahead. I told her I was looking at a foreclosure property online and was trying to locate the listing agent to get some information. She admitted she didn't know anything about the property but agreed to have the listing agent call later that evening.

Interestingly, she didn't bother to gather any information from me as a potential prospect.

About 30 minutes later, I received a second call, and this time it was from the actual listing agent—which should have been progress, you might guess, but not so much. She, too, had no information to offer regarding the property. "What you know is what I know," she said. You might expect she would volunteer to do some homework on the property, but that didn't happen either. Nor did she ask me any questions to determine my interest or needs. Brilliant guy that I am, I started to detect a pattern.

Have you ever experienced a salesperson who asks a question in a negative light rather than from a positive perspective? Like this: "You don't want to buy something, do you?" I know, that probably sounds nuts, but salespeople are guilty of this more than you might imagine. In this case, the agent didn't say, "I'd be happy to show you the property," or ask, "May I meet you at the property so you can inspect it?" Instead, she said, "Do you want me to show you the property?"

I'm probably just being critical. After all, she could have asked, "You don't want to see the property, do you?"

Anyway, we made an appointment to see the house the very next morning, so my wife and I jumped in the car and made the short drive, speculating some about the property and some about the agent. As we approached the home, I noticed she was already parked in the driveway. Frankly, if she had been ten minutes late, it would have fit much better with my initial impressions, so I was pleasantly surprised. Maybe it was just late when she called, I thought, and she wasn't quite on her game.

Clearly, I'm a glass-half-full kind of guy.

Unfortunately, when we introduced ourselves, she did not appear to be in any way half-full. Or even one-quarter full. She had no notebook. No business card. No information. Nothing. She certainly didn't look the part of a professional (she was wearing sweat pants), nor did she act the part of a professional.

Overlooking her rather casual appearance, we went in to investigate the property. In the 20 minutes we were there, I believe she asked exactly one question: "How do you plan to pay for the property? Cash?" she asked. Nope. Just a typical mortgage.

"Hmm," she replied. "You're gonna need an approval letter." Approval letter? I guess if you venture out to look at foreclosure properties you're expected to know these things, but I was lost. I didn't know where to get one or why it was needed, and she didn't offer to explain. However, after several questions, I finally got an idea of what was required, though she never offered to help us obtain the letter, nor did she offer to walk us through the process.

I did mention several times that we were looking at properties for a specific reason, and you might have expected her to see an opportunity, but evidently she didn't. She never asked any questions or explored our needs in any way. She didn't suggest a plan for follow-up or next steps. Here I am—a qualified, eager prospect who, for all she knows, might do tons of business and/or refer her to dozens of potential clients—and you would think I was wasting her time.

In terms of marketing her future services, she failed miserably.

BECOME A RESOURCE

Very, very few salespeople can rely *only* on those customers they currently serve, so new prospects are a necessity—which suggests that one eye should always be on your current customer, and the other eye should always be roving, looking for the next opportunity. Whether those prospects present themselves as additional opportunities within a current account, or as a brand new opportunity elsewhere, you have to pay constant attention to your sales pipeline.

What that means is, when you're not selling, you should be *marketing*.

Of course, the most important and most effective marketing any salesperson ever does is embodied in one simple principle: do great work for your customers. To borrow from best-selling author and renowned management consultant, Ken Blanchard, your objective should be to create "Raving Fans." Why? Because Raving Fans are far more likely to use you when they need additional products or services, and they will almost assuredly refer you to others.

The other type of ongoing marketing activity to pursue is what I call *personal marketing*. Personal marketing is the intentional process of creating awareness of your value by becoming a resource to your customers and prospects.

Note that I'm not talking about radio or TV or billboards or websites or blogs, or any of the myriad of other promotional mechanisms available to a business. The marketing I am referring to is providing value to your customers and prospects outside of the products and services you provide.

In many cases, the very best example of personal marketing is the theme captured in Chapter 45, where I discuss how good ideas always open doors. Useful ideas will always increase your value to customers; however, ideas are just one of the many things that salespeople can use to become valuable resources to their customers and prospects.

Others include:

- Industry research

- White Papers

- Technology updates

- Economic information relative to your market

- Introductions to key people in your network

- Referrals to potential new customers, partners, or vendors

- Training for customer employees in your area(s) of expertise

- Joint sales calls with the customer's salespeople (if applicable)

Each of these items represents a value outside of your products or services. When you provide these items to prospects *before* asking for a sale, you not only market yourself as a resource to those potential customers, you capitalize on something called 'reciprocation'.

In his best-selling book *Influence: The Psychology of Persuasion*, Robert Cialdini reveals six powerful psychological principles of persuasion. One of those principles is the concept of reciprocation, the idea that human nature is powerfully motivated to respond positively to those who first provide them with something of value.

The converse is also true: when you try to sell something before you have earned the right or standing to ask for money, human nature is powerfully motivated to respond negatively. In other words, it is always in your best interest, and coincidentally, in the best interest of your customers, for you to give value first.

Let's go back to the real estate agent in my story above. Think about the many resources she might have provided in marketing her services:

- A packet of information on how to buy foreclosure properties

- A list of properties similar to those we were considering, including a map showing the locations relevant to our residence

- A list of municipal contacts for property inspections, construction permits, and so on

- A list of key websites that discuss home renovation, remodeling, or flipping houses

- An introduction to one or more reliable subcontractors (electrical, plumbing, finish carpenters, painters, etc.)

- An introduction to an expert in foreclosure properties

- A referral to a mortgage specialist or a title company

Before you proceed any further, develop a comprehensive list of potential resources you might provide to customers.

1-on-1 Principle™
When you want to build strong business relation-ships, provide value first without asking for anything in return.

CHAPTER 42

AVOIDING ELEVATORS

"Forget words like 'hard sell' and 'soft sell.' That will only confuse you. Just be sure your advertising is saying something with substance, something that will inform and serve the consumer, and be sure you're saying it like it's never been said before.
— *William Bernbach*

"The single biggest problem in communication is the illusion that it has taken place."
— *George Bernard Shaw*

A FEW YEARS AGO, I spoke to a state association of personnel consultants. Prior to my presentation, the president of the association asked the meeting attendees to introduce themselves and briefly describe their specialties or primary areas of work.

The first person stood, introduced himself, and offered this description of his firm's services: "We specialize in placing engineers."

The next person followed the same routine and described his services this way: "We specialize in the placement of administrative staff and accounting personnel."

The third person decided to raise the bar even further: "We specialize in executive placement, IT staffing, back-office legal personnel, and other administrative staff."

And so it went; each person accepting the implied challenge and adding to the length of "specialties" until the last person introduced himself and said, "Really, we specialize in just about everything."

Which qualifies as a world-class oxymoron. And I was the only person who appeared to think it was funny. Specialize in everything? I almost choked.

Much has been written about the concept of an "elevator speech." It is purported to be a brief presentation—60 seconds or so—that is specifically designed to give someone a compelling view of you, your company, and the products or services you provide. The idea is that you could deliver a verbal snapshot of your work in the short time you would spend in an elevator.

My suggestion? Stay out of elevators; 98 percent of the elevator speeches I have ever heard range from cheesy to nonsensical to downright insulting. Not only is the actual content typically poor, the delivery will make you cringe. Many sound like bad television commercials ("But wait!! There's more!!!"). Others are so full of four-syllable business words you don't have the first clue what they really do.

Listening to the average elevator speech makes me feel like I'm watching the first few episodes of the new season of *American Idol*. The ones in which you have to endure the really uncomfortable performances by people who are completely unaware of their lack of talent.

Awkward.

Here is a dandy:

> We assist companies in discovering the essence of their branding position, while helping them craft a singularly innovative and introspective verbal audition of their value proposition.

Translation: We write elevator speeches.

ENTHUSIASM SELLS

People mean well. They really do. They want to be unique and interesting. Instead of telling people they sell insurance or cars or paint or software or whatever, they want to create further interest that leads to a conversation. They want to rise above the mundane.

But it isn't working; in fact, it has backfired. The delivery is stilted. The language is contrived. Sadly, the classic elevator speech most closely resembles a dumpster fire.

However, there is still a problem: You are always going to meet new people, and those people are always going to ask you what you do. So, how do you reply? "I'm a salesperson"? When someone hears, or even infers, that you are in sales, they typically check to see if they still have a wallet, and they start looking for an exit out of the conversation.

So what's a poor salesperson to do? How do you overcome the resistance to the perceptions people have of selling?

The answer is simple: enthusiasm. People love genuine passion. It is very hard to walk away from someone who has an authentic zeal for what they do. In fact, one of the best definitions of selling I have ever heard is this: Selling is the transference of passion.

The truth is, if you're doing something you absolutely love to do, selling it in a 60-second introduction is not as difficult as you think. Think about the aspects of your company, your company culture, and the people you work with that you really enjoy—and then talk about it. Here is an example that will help you create your own ideas:

> "I am really fortunate. I work for a great company and I love it! I've been there six years now, and it has been quite an experience! What we sell is software, which certainly doesn't make us unique. But, what makes us unique is . . . ."

There you go. You can dress up the first part with your own heartfelt impressions of your company. The more you can share about the positive things that your company represents for you personally, the more connection you are likely to create with your listener. Why? Because it is refreshing to hear from people who enjoy what they do, and it is compelling to learn that people are enthusiastic about their jobs!

So, after a brief narrative about how much you enjoy your work, your company, or the people you work with every day, you tell your listener what you sell. You specifically say "which doesn't make us unique" because there are competitors who sell what you sell.

However, your competitors are not like you. So, you immediately follow up with, "But, what makes us unique is . . . ." And they will be ready to listen. They will want to hear the rest of the story.

Just don't use the language from that horrid elevator speech or you will ruin it.

> **1-on-1 Principle**™
> Avoid cheesy elevator speeches like the plague.

CHAPTER 43

TALENT IS OVERRATED

"Our goals can only be reached through a vehicle of a plan, in which we must fervently believe, and upon which we must vigorously act. There is no other route to success."

— Pablo Picasso

"The general who loses a battle makes but few calculations beforehand. Thus do many calculations lead to victory, and few calculations to defeat: how much more no calculation at all! It is by attention to this point that I can foresee who is likely to win or lose."

— Sun Tzu, The Art of War

ON JANUARY 7, 2013, Nick Saban coached the University of Alabama football team to its third BCS championship victory in four years. In only six years as the Crimson Tide's head coach, Saban has averaged better than ten wins each season, claimed three Southeast Conference titles, and hoisted the Coaches' Trophy (national champions) three times.

And, if that's not enough, he has a national championship as head coach of LSU to boot. Four national titles in an arena where a single championship is the pinnacle of a coaching career.

Why do some people consistently succeed where others consistently fall short? How are some people able, time and again, to reach the top of their given profession? Undoubtedly, there are a number of key factors that have contributed to Saban's success as a college football head coach, but I suspect that none are more important than his attention to *planning and preparation*. In his *CNN Money* article, entitled "Leadership Lessons from Nick Saban," author Brian O'Keefe explains:

What really separates Saban from the crowd is his organizational modus operandi. In Tuscaloosa they call it the Process. It's an approach he implemented first in turnarounds at Michigan State and LSU and seems to have perfected at Alabama. **He has a plan for everything.** He has a detailed program for his players to follow, and he's highly regimented. Above all, Saban keeps his players and coaches focused on execution—yes, another word for process—rather than results.

A plan for everything? Detailed program? Highly regimented? Who knew success could be so much...work? Obviously, this approach works for Saban, but it's hardly a pattern, is it? After all, aren't there many paths to success?

Turns out, Saban is hardly unique in his approach. Consider the legendary Paul "Bear" Bryant, who also coached at Alabama. In his 25-year tenure, Bryant led 'Bama to six national championships and thirteen conference titles. He also considered planning to be the cornerstone of his success:

If you want to coach you have three rules to follow to win. One, surround yourself with people who can't live without football. I've had a lot of them. Two, be able to recognize winners. They come in all forms. And, three, **have a plan for everything.**

Get the idea? Bryant, like his future counterpart, Nick Saban, believed that planning was the key to success. In fact, he believed the *one* thing that consistently sets winners apart from the pack was preparation: "Follow the plan and you'll be surprised how successful you can be," he once observed. "Most people don't have a plan. That's why it's easy to beat most folks."

THE GREAT EQUALIZER

In 2010, Geoffrey Colvin, *Fortune's* senior editor-at-large, published a book entitled, *Talent is Overrated: What Really Separates World-Class*

Performers from Everybody Else. It is a fascinating book, and one that provides tremendous inspiration and hope for all of us "regular" salespeople:

> Salespeople make attractive subjects for researchers because at least they produce something clear to measure: sales. There may still be endless sources of noise in the results, as salespeople explain eloquently to their bosses, but over time and over large numbers of subjects, most of that should wash out.
>
> In this analysis of analyses, the researchers found that if you ask salespeople's bosses to rate them, the ratings track intelligence moderately well; bosses tend to think that smarter salespeople are better. **But when the researchers compared intelligence with actual sales results, they found nothing.** (emphasis added)

The cynical (or the sarcastic) might decide this explains why there are so many bad salespeople in the world. The right conclusion is that it explains why companies have historically hired so many bad salespeople—they were looking for all the wrong things. The tendency is to look for smart people with outgoing personalities. Much better from my perspective to look for good planning skills and the perseverance to overcome a myriad of obstacles.

As a young salesman, one of my sales managers constantly hammered this simple theme into my head: *Plan your work. Work your plan.* He wore it out. Every sales meeting: Plan your work. Work your plan.

This was the very same guy who was always reminding us that selling is the highest paid hard work there is and the lowest paid easy work there is. Both ideas gave me hope. I may not have been the smartest guy around, or the most talented, but I could *work*. I could plan. I could prepare. And in doing so, as Bear Bryant suggested, I could beat most folks.

The irony is that most salespeople hate planning. Most even hate the *idea* of planning. In fact, my experience has been that most salespeople would rather do *anything* else. Learn a new networking technique? Sure. A fancy new power close? You bet. A flashy new transition for the presentation slide deck? Cool.

But planning? Seriously?

You bet. Planning is the great equalizer. In sports. In battle. In business. In any activity where a distinction is drawn between winning and losing. Sun Tzu, the 6th century Chinese general and strategist said it well: "Thus do many calculations lead to victory, and few calculations to defeat."

1-on-1 Principle™
Consistent success depends on a good plan and your willingness to work that plan.

CHAPTER 44

FROM HERE TO THERE

"He who every morning plans the transaction of the day and follows out that plan, carries a thread that will guide him through the maze of the most busy life. But where no plan is laid, where the disposal of time is surrendered merely to the chance of incidence, chaos will soon reign."

— *Victor Hugo*

"Being busy does not always mean real work. The object of all work is production or accomplishment, and to either of these ends there must be forethought, system, planning, intelligence, and honest purpose, as well as perspiration. Seeming to do is not doing."

— *Thomas A. Edison*

DAVID ALLEN IS RECOGNIZED as the world's leading authority on personal and organizational productivity. His best-selling book, *Getting Things Done: The Art of Stress-Free Productivity*—which has created a vast army of "GTD" devotees and spawned over 160 electronic and web-based task management applications—has sold over 1.5 million copies since its release in 2001. Allen's approach to productivity is pretty simple: Get organized. Get a plan. Get busy.

Of course, there are a whole lot of details in between, but the essence is pretty simple. Instead of getting organized and creating a plan, however, most people jump right out into the middle of the street—and wonder where all the traffic came from. This leads inevitably to what most of us would call crisis management and what Allen refers to as the Reactive Planning Model:

> But what happens if you don't plan ahead of time? In many cases, crisis! ("Didn't you get the tickets? I thought you were going to do that?!") Then, when the urgency of the last minute is upon you, the reactive planning model ensues.

What's the first level of focus when the stuff hits the fan? *Action!* Work harder! Overtime! More people! Get busier! And a lot of stressed-out people are thrown at the situation.

Then, when having a lot of busy people banging into each other doesn't resolve the situation, someone gets more sophisticated says, "We need to get *organized!*"

Sounds very much like a quarterly sales review when a salesperson is only 75 percent of forecast and the sales manager goes ballistic: "You need to make more calls! You need to make more presentations! You need to get organized!"

As Allen demonstrates, this is completely backwards. First, you need to figure out what you are trying to accomplish. Then, you need to brainstorm the ideas that will help you get there. Finally, you need a step-by-step plan to implement your ideas.

The point here is that a plan isn't haphazardly thrown together. There are many salespeople who claim to believe in planning and many who actually think they have a plan. But a simple (or even complex) To-Do list is not necessarily a plan; it's simply a list of tasks to be accomplished. The critical question is whether or not those tasks were created in reaction to external problems, or if they are a defined set of steps proactively created to achieve a defined objective.

There are a number of things that are believed to be a plan that aren't:

- Working harder is not a plan.

- Making more calls is not a plan.

- A revenue goal is not a plan.

- Being the best is not a plan.

A plan is a defined set of activities that is specifically designed to accomplish a clear objective. A plan is like a road map that details how a traveler intends to get from one location (here) to another location (there).

YOUR STRATEGIC SALES PLAN

In Chapters 14 through 16 , I outlined a methodology for identifying high-value, high-probability prospects in the planning phase of the sales process. But now that you have a stable full of great prospects, you need a different kind of plan, one that organizes your approach to protecting your KEY accounts and creates a step-by-step approach for developing your TARGET accounts. You need a strategic plan for developing your sales business.

This may sound like a daunting task, but the three elements of a strategic sales plan are really very straightforward:

1. Analyze your current situation (Where are you now?).

2. Determine your objectives (Where are you going?).

3. Create of map of your journey (How do you get there?).

It's just like planning a trip. That makes steps 1 and 2 critical because a trip can change dramatically based on where you start and where you intend to finish. A trip to Los Angeles that starts in New York City looks a lot different than one that begins in San Diego. The cross-country trip takes more time, more money, more stops. And more preparation.

For example, if your sales revenue last year was $10 million, what would your objective be this year? Clearly, I have no idea since I know nothing about your current situation, but I strongly suspect that your revenue goal will be much different than the salesperson whose total sales last year was only $500,000.

1. Where Are You Now?

First, you must create a clear picture of where you are now. Although you may discover others areas of assessment unique to your industry, here are some of the common items that need to be a part of your analysis:

- Current sales revenue

- Year-over-year sales growth (or decline)

- Current customer base (your 80/20 analysis)

- Distribution of customer base (by territory geography and/or by market segment)

- Current product mix (Where are you strong? Weak?)

- Margins for each product segment

- Number of new customers (Which product segments?)

- Number of customers lost (and why)

- Impact of new products or new marketing efforts

The idea here, as in any conventional business analysis, is to complete a thorough SWOT analysis of your current sales situation. Determine your current **strengths** and **weaknesses**. Identify the best possible **opportunities** to grow your business. Then, identify any potential external **threats** to your success. Each of these four areas will provide necessary input to your sales plan.

For example, if you're weak in a particular product line, can you boost sales by focusing on that product line with a specific group of accounts?

Do you need to develop more penetration (sell additional products and services) in specific accounts? If you're selling one or two products to a customer, could you be selling four or five or six? Are you failing to develop other departments, or business units, or locations?

Are parts of your sales territory underdeveloped? Are you spending too much time with smaller customers and failing to develop more substantial customers?

These and many other questions need to be answered, but once you have a grasp on your current situation, it's time to decide what you can reasonably accomplish over the next 12 months.

2. Where Are You Going?

The question here is what are your goals? After you have gained a clear understanding of your current sales efforts, it should be easy to create three to five specific sales objectives. Here are examples:

- Increase total sales revenue to _____

- Achieve my assigned sales objective, or exceed my assigned sales objective by _____

- Add _____ new accounts each quarter

- Increase gross margins in each new account by _____ percent

- Increase sales of Product X by _____ percent.

- Develop _____ new KEY accounts from my TARGET account list

Another place you might want to start is to consider a specific income objective. How much money do you want to make this year? By starting with an income objective, you can work backwards to arrive at concrete sales objectives that will ensure you meet your income goal. It is simple mathematics.

For example, if you aspire to make $100,000 in total compensation and your base salary is $60,000, you need $40,000 in additional bonuses and/or commissions to reach your goal. Let's assume that commissions on new product sales are 10 percent and you get a $5,000 bonus for achieving specific revenue objectives. That means you need $350,000 in new revenue, and you need to achieve 100 percent of plan to reach your target income.

The question is how to get there.

3. How Will You Get There?

This is where the actual plan gets developed. Now, however, you have the basis for a plan. You know where the starting line is, and you know where you want to go. Using the simple example above: How do you generate $350,000 in new revenue next year?

- In which accounts can you add revenue?

- Which products will you focus on?

- In which accounts can you increase sales?

- How many *new* accounts do you need to produce?

- Which market segments should you focus on?

- How many TARGET accounts will you need to develop?

- **Do you have enough opportunities in your pipeline to even produce the revenue you want?**

The last question is the single most important question to consider. In all of my experience, the single greatest predictor of whether or not you achieve your sales or income goal is the value of potential opportunities in your pipeline. Too many salespeople are trying to achieve a revenue objective with an insufficient number of opportunities currently in process.

However, it's difficult to know if you have enough opportunities until you decide what your revenue objective will be. It's like trying to determine if you have enough gasoline in the car for the trip—something you won't know until you determine where you want to go.

If you discover that your pipeline of opportunities is not sufficient to reach your goals, that knowledge becomes another critical piece of information in the assessment of your current situation. It also means that one of your primary goals will be to fill that pipeline to a point where you have the opportunity to reach your objectives.

Once again, the question is how to get there, and we're right back to Step 3 once again.

> **1-on-1 Principle™**
> A To-Do list is not a sales plan. A strategic plan requires a clear understanding of where you are, where you're going, and how you intend to get there.

CHAPTER 45

THE HOUSE EDGE

"Time is free, but it is priceless. You can't own it, but you can use it.
You can't keep it, but you can spend it. Once you've lost it
you can never get it back."
— *Harvey Mackay*

"Until you value yourself, you won't value your time. Until you value
your time, you will not do anything with it."
— *M. Scott Peck*

LET'S FACE IT, for the most part, the playing field in the sales profession is fairly level. The players are certainly not all the same, but the field generally isn't slanted in anyone's favor. For example, there are few, if any, technical advantages to be had. Competition is a constant. Every industry is affected by the ebb and flow of the economy. Day in and day out, from one industry to the next, the challenges are roughly all the same. Unreasonable customer demands. Resistance to change. The inability to get in front of decision makers.

So, you need an edge, and if you're any kind of competitor at all, you're always looking for something. A new, improved product. A better warranty program. Updated marketing material. An innovative promotion. Something—anything—that can tilt the scales in your favor.

The irony is that the most significant advantage you can claim is right underneath your nose. It is an edge that can easily vault you to the top of your profession—and it is hidden in plain sight.

In a casino, that slight advantage is called the "House Edge." It's the difference between the true odds of winning a given bet and the odds that the casino pays you when you win. Casinos are cash machines because they always pocket a small percentage of a winning bet (typically, one to five percent, but sometimes much more). It's a built-in advantage that guarantees success.

Wouldn't that be something? Is it possible for you to create a House Edge? Can you tip the scales slightly in your favor? The answer is simple: yes, you can. It is possible to create a definitive advantage for yourself, and it is right there for the taking. Here it is: when you learn to value your time for the perishable commodity it is, and therefore choose to manage it far more effectively, you will create a tangible advantage for yourself.

Why? Because more time means more sales calls, more conversations that lead to valuable information, more opportunities to develop important relationships, and more opportunities to develop KEY accounts, and on and on. If you're skeptical or, more likely, not at all convinced, let me ask you one very simple question:

> *If you had eight more hours every week that no other competitor had— the equivalent of one extra day each and every week—what kind of advantage would it give you?*

Eight hours per week = 96 minutes per day. Just a touch over an hour-and-a-half of extra time every single day of every single week. If available, it would represent an enormous advantage!

Still thinking that sounds ridiculous? Let me assure you that most salespeople give that much time away every day quite consistently. Not all, but most. As a general rule, salespeople are terrible time managers!

Here is a simple, straightforward way to pick up an extra eight hours per week. Trim 15 minutes each day from the following six areas and you will quickly "discover" an extra 90 minutes a day:

- Unnecessary phone calls
- Long lunches
- Unnecessary drive time
- Poor call planning

- Administrative tasks that can be done after hours

- Busy work that is really unproductive or unnecessary

The sad thing is that I have known salespeople who willingly give away those eight hours per week; in fact, they have demanded to give them away! They believe they need an entire 'office day' each week just to do administrative work. Budgets. Expense reports. Call reports. Responses to proposals. You name it. If you can cut that time in half, you pick up four hours right away. Do all that work after hours or on weekends and you pick up the full eight hours all at once.

Understand this: time is the real currency that salespeople trade in. Salespeople never, ever have enough time, and the old adage is true: *Time is money!* As I mentioned in Chapter 12, every hour wasted is an hour that cannot be recaptured or reused productively. Every hour lost is time that won't be spent in front of potential customers.

With that in mind, look around and observe how incredibly cavalier we are with our time!

WORK WITH PURPOSE

Managing your time effectively means working with purpose. It means that most everything you do is done for a specific reason with a specific objective in mind. It also means that one of your primary objectives is to eliminate, as much as possible, those things that waste your most valuable resource. Among other things, it means creating a *weekly* call plan. Think about this: how would it impact your time management if, before you left home on Monday morning, you knew exactly where you were going to go that week, who you were going to see, and what you expected to accomplish?

I understand that you may not have every appointment filled for the week, but it means that you have planned sales activity in specific areas and that you have very specific objectives in mind. You've given thought to each day and the things you must do to reach your objectives.

The same can be said for each individual sales call. Effective time management means every call needs to count; it needs to produce a result. In planning a sales call, you should have very distinct objectives for the call:

- Who am I seeing?

- What is the objective of this call?

- What information do I need to acquire?

- Who else do I need to meet?

- What will I do if I get there and the prospect is unexpectedly unavailable?

Zig Ziglar had a label for this type of effective time management. He called it the "day-before-vacation-attitude." He points out that people can get all kinds of things done the day before they leave on vacation simply because they know it has to be done. So, they create a step-by-step plan to make it happen.

Stop the mail. Go to the bank. Talk to the neighbors. Wash the clothes you want to take. Pack the suitcases. Buy a swim suit. Take the dog to the kennel. Get the oil changed in the car. Get the kids packed. Who knows what else. All that, typically on the day before you leave for vacation.

As a salesperson, you will be amazed at what you can accomplish if you take the same approach to managing your time. An extra eight hours a week, properly used, will make you a whole lot of money.

1-on-1 Principle™
Effective time management provides the edge you need to achieve your sales objectives.

CHAPTER 46

ARE YOU A PROFESSIONAL VISITOR?

"What's the most resilient parasite? An idea. A single idea from the human mind can build cities. An idea can transform the world and rewrite all the rules."
— *From the film Inception*

"All the forces in the world are not so powerful as an idea whose time has come."
— *Victor Hugo*

LIKE MOST OTHER FAMILIES, ours has developed a host of holiday traditions over the years; things we do year after year that have become woven into the fabric of our holidays.

Many years ago, my son, Scott, started one of those, uh...different traditions, which has since become legendary at our house. When he was still a young boy (he's now 21 years old), he started using duct tape to wrap his Christmas gifts. Not Scotch® tape. Duct tape. Every year, Mom, Dad, Brother, and Sister always knew exactly which gifts under the Christmas tree were from Scott.

Have you ever tried to open a gift wrapped in duct tape?

In recent years, Scott has sold out completely to the holiday season. Instead of silver duct tape, he now uses red and green tape in various combinations of Houdini-like gift wrapping. It's bizarre; we actually look forward to seeing what the latest innovation in duct-tape decoration will look like.

Think for a minute about duct tape. How many different applications have you seen for that product? I've seen car repairs done with duct tape. Duct tape helped save the Apollo 13 astronauts. Clearly, duct tape makes a suitable substitute for wrapping paper. Duct tape is just one of those products that inevitably lead to new ideas and new applications.

Most products are like that in one way or another. They generate new ideas, new applications, and, many times, spin off new opportunities.

Social media provides a vivid example. It seems like every other day there is a new idea that is spun off from an existing social media application. There was MySpace and LinkedIn. Then Facebook. Then Twitter. And YouTube. And Blogger and Typepad. And Flickr. And Pinterest. And Instagram. And that's just the ones most people are aware of; there are scores of others. Although one application didn't necessarily lead directly to another, each of these platforms deals with two common ideas—community and social sharing.

Recently, however, people have begun to realize the potential long-term problems associated with content so readily shared on the Internet. Compromising pictures, hasty status updates, online rants and the like, once shared, can come back to haunt you. As is usually the case, this problem led to an idea that ultimately resulted in a new solution—Snapchat.

Snapchat is a social media application that allows users to share messages and pictures, but once viewed for a few seconds, they disappear. It's social sharing with a time limit. "It became clear how awful social media is," said one of Snapchat's founders, Evan Spiegel, 22. "There is real value in sharing moments that don't live forever."

That one idea formed a company that has attracted millions of users and has already been valued at $60 million.

What's next?

THE VALUE OF AN IDEA

Ideas are what make salespeople exceptionally valuable. Typically, if the only thing you provide your customers is a product or a service, then you will always be seen as little more than a "salesperson." However, if you can become a source of innovative applications of your product or service or other ideas that benefit your customers, your value multiplies many times over.

Suddenly, you're not just a salesperson, you are a valued partner.

This is one of the tremendous benefits of becoming an expert in your field. You will become aware of new product or service applications, and you will acquire important information on innovations and advancements within the industry. The knowledge that you accrue as a specialist in your field will prove invaluable in your relationships with customers.

To this end, you should also learn how other customers use your products or services. Great ideas often originate from the experiences of other customers and these ideas are great reasons to have meetings with your customers. Too many salespeople make calls on customers or prospects with little more to offer than "I'm just checking in to see how things are going."

If your notion of a good sales call is to show up and shoot the breeze, see how your buddies are doing, and ask if they've had a chance to look over your latest brochure or review your last proposal, you're not a professional salesperson. You, my friend, are a *professional visitor*, and customers simply don't have time for visitors.

Customers have their own fires to put out, their own problems to solve, and enough day-to-day challenges to keep them busy for a week. They typically don't have nearly enough time in the day to do what they need to get done, so they certainly don't have time to waste with salespeople. The reason most customers don't have the slightest interest in talking to salespeople is that they are notorious time-wasters, which becomes yet another advantage for salespeople who understand the importance of time.

Customers almost always have time for salespeople with valuable ideas. Next time you're having trouble deciding on how to approach a prospect, or if you're not sure what your call objective should be, look for a great idea to share.

Think "duct tape."

1-on-1 Principle™
Good ideas make you valuable far beyond the products and services you provide.

CHAPTER 47

WHAT IS A RELATIONSHIP WORTH?

"In sales and customer relations, the quality of your relationships will determine the outcome of events when there is a problem or issue with price, delivery, quality, or service."
— *Jeffrey Gitomer*

"I felt about as good as anybody would, sitting in a capsule on top of a rocket that were both built by the lowest bidder."
— *Astronaut John Glenn, as he awaited the launch into earth's orbit in 1962*

STRAPPED IN A SEAT ATOP an Atlas rocket contemplating a couple of laps around the earth is not the time you want to consider the consequences of your company having chosen the lowest priced vendor. It is, to say the very least, a sobering thought.

Unfortunately, in business-to-business (B2B) selling, it has come to be accepted truth that the only important factor in a buying decision is the *price* of the product or service to be purchased. That is what prospects tell salespeople every single day, and that is what those same salespeople, in turn, tell their sales managers.

Therefore, it must be true.

Except that it's not. People don't typically buy the lowest price; instead, they attempt to pay the lowest price possible for what they have decided they want. However, if a buyer has decided your product or service has nothing more or less to offer than your competitor's product, they will typically try to leverage each of you against the other to secure a better price. Worse, once you have allowed the prospect to convince you that your solution is just like everyone else's and the decision is going to be made on price, it is entirely too late to negotiate because you have nothing to negotiate.

What salespeople need to internalize is that unless you're selling junk, your product is worth far more than you think. Your product (or service) has much more value than even you give yourself credit for; the real problem is you haven't presented that value in a way that captures the prospect's attention.

A few years ago, I worked with a local distributor that sold supplies to metal fabrication companies. The owner of the business had hired a long-time industry sales veteran who promised that he would immediately and dramatically increase the company's sales. Years in the industry had allowed him to create close "relationships" with buyers throughout the region, and those relationships, he had guaranteed the owner, would allow him to rapidly become the top producer for the company.

And he did exactly that.

True to his word, in his first year, this salesperson delivered in a big way, adding new accounts and additional revenue on a steady basis. Unfortunately, there was one small problem: the gross margin percentage produced by his sales was *significantly* less than the other salespeople in the company.

The client was understandably concerned. A hefty sales increase required the company to obtain more resources—another delivery truck, another driver, more warehouse personnel, and so on—and those resources cost money. Predictably, the company struggled to accommodate the influx of new customers while continuing to provide the same level of service to its existing customers—a problem every rapidly growing company must contend with. However, in this case, the salesperson's lower margins meant that the company's resources were being churned much harder with very little additional marginal revenue to show for it.

With very few exceptions, salespeople don't bear the risks of ownership. They don't put capital at risk. They don't contend with the costs of operating the business. They simply live in the moment, trading products or services provided by the company for money provided by the customer. It is what makes selling such an incredible opportunity.

However, this same opportunity also provides a very real danger to a business owner—the possibility of abusing the privilege afforded to a salesperson. When salespeople indiscriminately lower prices in order to develop business, they are literally trading away the owner's money in order to create commissions for themselves. While this may be great for the salesperson, it's not so great for the company.

I wondered, in this case, if this was simply the initial cost of getting customers to switch to a new, unknown supplier. Perhaps the salesperson felt the need to offer an inducement to his existing customers to entice them into making a change, which can often be a bit scary for a customer.

So, I inquired as to why his margins were so much lower, which didn't go so well. He pointedly explained to me that the industry was very competitive (aren't they all?). Then, he made it clear that his customers could easily get a lower price from his competitors, and it was only his strong *relationships* that allowed him to get the business. Finally, he emphasized that *his* customers *deserved* a lower price since they could buy the products at a cheaper price elsewhere.

What?

So, Why Do I Need You?

Which leads us to an interesting question. Exactly what is a relationship worth?

Salespeople universally extol the value and necessity of creating relationships with customers, so what is the value of any given relationship? As the salesperson suggested above, do relationships serve only to provide the opportunity to compete for the lowest price?

If so, why does the company even need you? Why not eliminate the expense of salespeople altogether and simply advertise the lowest price, guaranteed?

After all, the alleged customer relationship has only created the opportunity to get the business with the lowest price, and if price really is what is truly important in the sale, why bother to hire people whose very responsibility is to educate and persuade customers? Especially when customers can use digital media to become completely educated on your products and services long before you arrive?

Unless, of course, there is much more to selling than just the price of the product.

In reality, showing a product, quoting a price, and subsequently competing on price is *not* selling, but salespeople who don't know how to create and sell the true value of their solutions wind up bargaining, not selling. And bargaining—or negotiating, or quibbling, or begging (in some rare cases)—is a losing proposition for a salesperson whose prospect has already decided that his solution is no different than his competitor's.

If you are simply a product-pusher who places the entire outcome of the sale on the price of your solution, your business relationships aren't really worth anything to you or your company.

Ask yourself these questions:

- What is less risk worth?

- What is responsiveness worth?

- What is trust worth?

The reality is that each of these things are critically important to customers, and most are willing to pay a little more for the peace of mind each of those items provides. In fact, here are a number of reasons why customers will pay companies a little more for a product or service:

- Because they trust the company

- Because they have confidence in the company

- Because they perceive less risk with the company

- Because they believe the company understands their business and what is important to them

- Because they value the service and support you provide in making change easier for their company

- Because they know the company's support people are helpful, cooperative, and easy to work with

- Because they know the company will take responsibility for the implementation of their solution, regardless of circumstances

- Because they have seen that the company can and will solve problems that other companies can't or won't

- Because they know the company has more resources available than their competitors

- Because they believe the company is *truly* responsive and will address issues very quickly

- Because they believe the company provides a value to them beyond the solution that is provided

- Because they appreciate a company that demonstrates genuine appreciation for their business

The truth is that customer relationships *are* important. However, the reason they are important is not because they give you the opportunity to get the business at a lower price. *Real* relationships are important because they lead to trust and confidence and mutual respect.

And those things are worth something to the customer.

1-on-1 Principle™
A genuine relationship earns you the right to something much more than a price quote.

1-on-1 Principles™

Chapter 41:
When you want to build strong business relationships, provide value first without asking for anything in return.

Chapter 42:
Avoid cheesy elevator speeches like the plague.

Chapter 43:
Consistent success depends on a good plan and your willingness to work that plan.

Chapter 44:
A To-Do list is not a sales plan. A strategic plan requires a clear understanding of where you are, where you're going, and how you intend to get there.

Chapter 45:
Effective time management provides the edge you need to achieve your sales objectives.

Chapter 46:
Good ideas make you valuable far beyond the products and services you provide.

Chapter 47:
A genuine relationship earns you the right to something much more than a price quote.

PART IX

THE ROAD AHEAD

CHAPTER 48

THE POTENTIAL FOR GREATNESS

"Dream no small dreams for they have no power to move
the hearts of men."

— *Goethe*

"Greatness is not a function of circumstance. Greatness, it turns out,
is largely a matter of conscious choice, and discipline."

— *Jim Collins*

WILMA RUDOLPH WON THREE gold medals in track and field at the 1960 Summer Olympics in Rome. Emerging from the games as 'the fastest woman on earth,' she was recognized as both the United Press Athlete of the Year and the Associated Press Woman Athlete of the Year. Her life, a remarkable journey from infantile paralysis to celebrated track athlete, is an inspiration to anyone who would remotely consider their background a deterrent to success.

Wilma was the twentieth of 22 children. Her family was indescribably poor. To complicate matters, Wilma suffered one childhood disease after another—scarlet fever, measles, mumps, chicken pox, and double pneumonia—but it was polio that left her handicapped. She was forced to wear a brace on her leg until the age of 12.

Finally, the brace came off and Wilma learned to walk normally again. It wasn't long before she took up basketball, and though she failed to play in a single game her first three years, she eventually emerged as a star and led her high school team to a state championship. It was not basketball, however, that would serve as her springboard to world-wide fame.

It was track.

In 1956, at the tender age of 16, her blazing speed earned her a spot on the women's Olympic 400-meter relay team in Melbourne, Australia. The women earned the bronze medal, but four years later,

Wilma became a household name. She won the 100-meter dash, the 200-meter dash, and led the 400-meter relay team to a world record, becoming the first American woman to win three gold medals in track and field.

SUCCESS IS NOT AN ACCIDENT

"We are all the same in this notion," Wilma once said. "The potential for greatness lives within each of us." No doubt this is true, but it takes enormous strength to overcome challenges and endure hardship. Often times, it's so much easier to blame something, or someone else, for our own failure.

In two decades of sales training, I have never found a salesperson who didn't want to make more money. I know because I ask. Not that money is the only thing that motivates people who sell for a living, but, without exception, each and every person I ask readily acknowledges his or her wish to bring home a fatter paycheck. Unfortunately, and this is a critical point for all aspiring sales professionals, only a few have actually been willing to do what it takes to make more money.

Only a very small percentage of salespeople who have claimed they want to make more money have been willing to commit the time, energy, and resources necessary to take their incomes to the next level. The rest prefer to blame circumstances or other people for their failure.

The truth, however, is that sales success is not dependent on or limited by race, gender, or socio-economic background. Personality style is irrelevant. No one is born to be a salesperson any more than they are born to be an accountant or a welder. Careers are simply chosen—based on one's background, skill sets, and personal enjoyment. But, as in any other career, the prerequisites to achieving one's dreams in the world of selling are simple: you must have an unwavering desire to learn the skills that are necessary to achieve those dreams, and you must have the discipline to practice and hone those skills until they can be executed flawlessly.

Both require that you accept your personal responsibility for your success or failure. Success is not an accident. Success is awarded to those who simply cannot live without it, to those who are willing to prepare and work and persist, despite all odds.

The truth is, if you cannot envision greatness, it will almost surely elude you.

1-on-1 Principle™
Everybody wants to be successful; only a few have what it takes.

Introduction

- Daniel H. Pink, *To Sell is Human: The Surprising Truth About Moving Others* (Riverhead Books, 2012).

Chapter 1

- The quote from Chris Gardner at the beginning of the chapter was taken from of an interview with Chris Gardner conducted by Geoffrey James (BNET, December 22, 2009). Retrieved from http://blogs.bnet.com/salesmachine/?p=7249&tag=col1;post-7249

- The details of Chris Gardner's life were assimilated from various newspaper articles and personal interviews as well as his autobiography, *The Pursuit of Happyness* (Harper Collins, 2006). A biographical film of the same name features Will Smith as Gardner, and Smith's real-life son, Jaden, as Chris Jr. (Columbia Pictures Corporation, Relativity Media, Overbrook Entertainment, 2006).

- Gardner eventually bought his own red Ferrari from basketball legend Michael Jordan. His vanity license plate reads "NOT MJ."

Chapter 2

- To win the Triple Crown in Major League Baseball is to finish the season as the leader in three statistical categories: home runs, batting average, and runs batted in (RBIs). Thirteen MLB players have won the Triple Crown, the most recent being Carl Yastrzemski of the Boston Red Sox, in 1967. Rogers Hornsby won the award twice, in 1922 and 1925, playing for the St. Louis Cardinals.

- Both quotes about Ted Williams were taken from "His Desire Made Wish Come True," by Bob Ryan, *Boston.com* (*The Boston Globe*), July 5, 2002. Retrieved from http://www.boston.com/ sports/redsox/williams/stories/his_desire_made_wish_come_tr ue.shtml

CHAPTER 3

- NBC, *The Biggest Loser* (2004). Created by Dave Broome, Mark Koops, and Benjamin Silverman. The show is produced by 25/7 Productions, and distributed by NBC Universal Television Distribution.

- In Season 9 of *The Biggest Loser*, contestant Michael Ventrella lost a record 264 pounds, 50.19 percent of his original body weight of 526 pounds. In losing 239 pounds, Danny lost 55.58 percent of his original bodyweight, a record that still stands.

- Danny Cahill, *Lose Your Quit: Achieving Success One Step at a Time* (Harrison House, 2013).

CHAPTER 4

- H.R. Chally Group research results taken from the *H.R. Chally World Class Sales Excellence Research Report*, by Howard Stevens and Sally Stevens (2007).

CHAPTER 6

- Joan Magretta, *Understanding Michael Porter: the Essential Guide to Competition and Strategy* (Harvard Business Press Books, 2011).

- M.P. Mueller, "How Do You Compete with FedEx and U.P.S?," *You're the Boss* (a *New York Times* blog), April 26, 2012. Retrieved from http://boss.blogs.nytimes.com/2012/04/26/how-do-you- compete-with-fedex-and-ups/

CHAPTER 7

- Quote taken from *The 7 Marketing Mistakes Every Business Makes*, by Terri Langhans (Blah Blah Blah Publishing, 2003). For more information, visit http://www.blahblahblah.us.

CHAPTER 10

- Information about The Flintco Companies taken from the corporate website (www.flinto.com), numerous industry sources, and the author's personal interview with CEO Tom Maxwell.

CHAPTER 11

- Lengthy quote regarding Dan Witkowski's ordeal taken from "Back from the Brink," by Elaine Porterfield, *Pacific Northwest: The Seattle Times Magazine*, January 9, 2005. Retrieved from http://seattletimes.nwsource.com/pacificnw/2005/0109/cover.html.

- Dan Witkowski quote take from "Dan Witkowski: Survivor. The loss of lower legs won't stop him," by Pat Muir, *Daily Record*, March 13, 2004. Retrieved from http://dailyrecordnews.com/news/article_b245de68-5f21-591f-a5f0-f434224b305c.html

- According to TraditionalMountaineering.org, the Four Basic Responsibilities of the Backcountry Traveler are (1) to tell a reliable person where you are going, what you are going to do and when you will return; (2) to be prepared with a light weight daypack and enough extra clothing, water, food and selected gear to survive an emergency stop of several hours or overnight; (3) to have a topographic map of the area and an inexpensive GPS that provides your coordinates; and (4) to carry your common digital cell phone and periodically learn where you can contact any cell towers. Retrieved from http://www.traditionalmountaineering.org/Basic.htm

- According to Traditionalmountaineering.org, The Ten Essentials include a map, compass, sunglasses and sunscreen, extra food and water, extra clothes, headlamp or flashlight, first aid kit, fire starter, matches and knife. Retrieved from http://www.traditional mountaineering.org/Essentials.htm

CHAPTER 13

- Quotation taken from *Higher: A Historic Race to the Sky and the Making of a City*, by Neal Bascomb (Broadway, 2004).

CHAPTER 14

- The terms "KEY" and "TARGET" (see Chapter 16) are excerpted from a model used at The Center for Sales Strategy, Inc. (www.csscenter.com) called the *Account List Management System*. I have used the 80/20 rule as a sales tool throughout most of my career, both as a salesperson and sales manager, and I found that the CSS model provides an excellent nomenclature for account stratification that fits perfectly with my sales approach.

CHAPTER 16

- The idea of the "Hedgehog Concept" is taken from *Good to Great: Why Some Companies Make the Leap...and Others Don't*, by Jim Collins (New York: Harper Collins, 2001), p. 98.

CHAPTER 17

- Quotation from Don Rainey taken from his January 2010 blog post, "The Top 5 Rookie Mistakes in Pitching VC's." Don is a general partner with Grotech Ventures, which has over $1 billion under management. Retrieved from: http://startups.typepad.com /my_weblog/2010/01/the-top-5-rookie-mistakes-in-pitching-vcs.html

CHAPTER 18

- *A Few Good Men* (1992). Written by Aaron Sorkin. Directed by Rob Reiner. Castle Rock Entertainment. Columbia Pictures. Script excerpt available at Internet Movie Script Database (IMSDb). Retrieved from http://www.imsdb.com/scripts/A-Few-Good-Men.html

CHAPTER 23

- Quote from John "Grizz" Deal taken from "On the Road With a Supersalesman," by David H. Freedman, *Inc.*, April 1, 2010. Retrieved from: http://www.inc.com/mag-azine/20100401/on-the-road-with-a-supersalesman.html

CHAPTER 24

- Quotes from Michael McLaughlin taken from "When Sales Questions Fail You," The Guerilla Consultant Newsletter, August 2009. To learn more about Michael and the services offered by Mindshare Consulting, visit www.mindshareconsulting.com.

CHAPTER 25

- Quote from *Seinfeld* taken from Episode 167, "The Dealership." Created by Larry David and Jerry Seinfeld. Produced by Shapiro/ West Productions in association with Castle Rock Entertainment. Distributed (since 2002) by Sony Pictures Television.

- Quote taken from "Baldwin Resigns as USOC President," by Alan Abrahamson, *Los Angeles Times*, May 25, 2002.

CHAPTER 26

- Information and quotes from Jim Koch taken from "How Sam Adams Founder Jim Koch is Helping Entrepreneurs Brew the

American Dream," by Shawn Parr, *Fast Company*, February 24, 2012.

- Main quote from Jim Koch taken from "The View from the Field," *Harvard Business Review*, July-August 2012, p. 103.

Chapter 27

- Quote from USC head coach Lane Kiffin taken from "USC's Matt Barkley shows his loyalty by returning for senior year," by Greg Logan, *Newsday*, September 6, 2012. Retrieved from http://www.newsday.com/sports/college/college-football/usc-s-matt-barkley-shows-his-loyalty-by-returning-for-senior-year-1.3960819.

- Zig Ziglar quotation taken from his book *Ziglar on Selling: The Ultimate Handbook for the Complete Sales Professional* (Thomas Nelson, 1991), p. 96.

Chapter 30

- Quote taken from "The Millenials Are Coming," *CBSNews*, February 11, 2009. Retrieved from http://www.cbsnews.com/2100-18560_1623475200.html?pageNum=3&tag=contentMain;contentBody

- Quote from John "Grizz" Deal taken from "On the Road With a Supersalesman," by David H. Freedman, *Inc.*, April 1, 2010. Retrieved from: http://www.inc.com/mag-azine/20100401/on-the-road-with-a-supersalesman.html

Chapter 32

- Quote from Kevin Allen taken from "Win the Pitch: Tips from MasterCard's 'Priceless' Pitchman," *Harvard Business Review*, May 8, 2012. Retrieved from http://blogs.hbr.org/cs/2012/05/mastering_the_art_of_the_pitch.html

Chapter 34

- Elisabeth Bumiller, "We Have Met the Enemy and He is Power-Point," *New York Times*, April 26, 2010. Retrieved from http://www.nytimes.com/2010/04/27/world/27powerpoint.html

- Read Seth Godin's blog post, "Really Bad PowerPoint," at http://sethgodin.typepad.com/seths_blog/2007/01/really_bad_powe.html. Download a PDF of the presentation at www.sethgodin.com/freeprize/reallybad-1.pdf

- Garr Reynolds, *Presentation Zen: Simple Ideas on Presentation Design and Delivery* (New Riders, 2008).

- Cliff Atkinson, *Beyond Bullet Points* (Microsoft Press, 2005).

Chapter 35

- Quotes from Chip and Dan Heath taken from their book *Made to Stick: Why Some Ideas Survive and Others Die* (Random House, 2007), p. 234.

Chapter 36

- Quotes from Jack Malcolm taken from his book *Strategic Sales Presentations* (Booktrope Editions, 2012).

- Quotes from Peter Gruber taken from his book *Tell to Win: Connect, Persuade, and Triumph with the Power of Story* (Crown Publishing Group, 2011), pp. 21-22.

Chapter 38

- ESPN Films 30-for-30, *"There's No Place Like Home,"* directed by Maura Mandt and Josh Swade. First aired October 16, 2012 on ESPN.

CHAPTER 39

- The two quotations in italics are taken from the movie *Caddyshack* (Orion Pictures, 1980). Directed by Harold Ramis.

CHAPTER 40

- Information on 'sales effectiveness' taken from *Achieve Sales Excellence: The 7 Customer Rules for Becoming the New Sales Professional,* by Howard Stevens and Theodore Kinni's (Platinum Press, 2006).

CHAPTER 41

- "Raving Fans" is the brainchild of the late Ken Blanchard (www.kenblanchard.com). He wrote an international best seller about creating legendary customer service entitled *Raving Fans: A Revolutionary Approach to Customer Service* (HarperCollins, 1993).

- Robert B. Cialdini is Regents' Professor Emeritus of Psychology and Marketing at Arizona State University, and author of *Influence: The Psychology of Persuasion* (Quill, Revised Edition 1993).

CHAPTER 43

- Nick Saban coached the LSU Tigers to an NCAA national championship in 2003.

- Quote about Nick Saban taken from "Leadership Lessons from Nick Saban," by Brian O'Keefe, *CNN Money*, September 7, 2012.

- Quotation taken from *Talent is Overrated: What Really Separates World-Class Performers from Everybody Else*, by Geoff Colvin (Portfolio Trade, 2010), p. 42.

CHAPTER 44

- Quotation taken from *Getting Things Done: The Art of Stress-Free Productivity*, by David Allen (Penguin Books, 2002), pp. 61-62

CHAPTER 45

- Zig Ziglar has presented the "day-before-vacation-attitude" in hundreds of live presentations, in a number audio and video recordings, and in his book *Over the Top* (Thomas Nelson, Inc., 1997).

CHAPTER 46

- Information about Snapchat and the quote from Evan Spiegel taken from "A Growing App Lets You See It, Then You Don't," by Jenna Wortham, *New York Times*, February 8, 2013. Retrieved from http://www.nytimes.com/2013/02/09/technology/snap-chat-a-growing-app-lets-you-see-it-then-you-dont.html?nl=todaysheadlines&emc=edit_ee_20130209&_r=0

CHAPTER 48

- Information regarding Wilma Rudolph taken from the book *Wilma Rudolph*, by Amy Ruth (Lerner Publications, 1999), and from a *Biography.com* article retrieved from http://www.biography.com/people/wilma-rudolph-9466552.

ABOUT THE AUTHOR

KELLY RIGGS is an author, speaker, and business performance coach for executives and companies throughout the United States, and he is widely recognized as a powerful speaker and dynamic trainer in the fields of leadership, sales development, and strategic planning. He is also a former two-time national Salesperson-of-the-Year with over two decades of sales management and sales training experience, including the development of two corporate sales training programs in two different industries.

Kelly's first book, *1-on-1 Management: What Every Great Manager Knows That You Don't*, was released in 2008. To obtain a copy, visit www.1on1Management.com.

·····················

To inquire about Kelly speaking at your association or corporate event, or training or coaching your sales team, email him at kelly@vmaxpg.com.

Vmax Performance Group
Transforming potential into performance.™
www.vmaxpg.com

Social Media:
Website: www.1on1selling.com
Twitter: @kellyriggs
LinkedIn: http://www.linkedin.com/in/kriggs
Facebook: http://www.facebook.com/VMaxPG
YouTube: http://www.youtube.com/user/kellysriggs